"They went in the top of my head . . ."

One night, I was lying in bed, and I had my back to the wall, when I saw these two aliens off towards the back of my head. I saw them come through the wall. And they came up to me. I didn't try to move. I don't know if there was any sensation. I remember just lying there. And they came over and they went in the top of my head. And it felt very good, so I allowed it. I perceived that I allowed it.

And they were slender. They were iridescent, like a whitish color. And that was that.

Pat Brown
UFO abductee

Pat Brown assumed her experience with extraterrestrials had come to an end. She didn't know that her ordeal had only just begun . . .

Extraterrestrial Visitations: True Accounts of Contact presents real accounts of very close contact with UFOs. Told in the witnesses' own words, the stories have immediacy, objectivity, and credibility. Revealed in these stories is the full spectrum—positive and negative—of the most perplexing mystery of modern times.

About the Author

Preston Dennett (California) is a field investigator for the Mutual UFO Network (MUFON). He is the author of *UFO Healings, One in Forty: The UFO Epidemic,* and *UFOs Over Topanga Canyon.* He has worked with the television programs *Sightings, National Geographic Explorer,* and *Encounters.*

To Write to the Author

If you wish to contact the author or would like more information about this book, please write to the author in care of Llewellyn Worldwide and we will forward your request. Both the author and publisher appreciate hearing from you and learning of your enjoyment of this book and how it has helped you. Llewellyn Worldwide cannot guarantee that every letter written to the author can be answered, but all will be forwarded. Please write to:

Preston Dennett
℅ Llewellyn Worldwide
P.O. Box 64383, Dept. 1-56718-220-8
St. Paul, MN 55164-0383, U.S.A.

Please enclose a self-addressed stamped envelope for reply,
or $1.00 to cover costs. If outside U.S.A., enclose
international postal reply coupon.

Many of Llewellyn's authors have websites with additional information and resources. For more information, please visit our website at http://www.llewellyn.com.

PRESTON DENNETT

EXTRATERRESTRIAL VISITATIONS

True Accounts of Contact

2001
Llewellyn Publications
St. Paul, Minnesota 55164-0383, U.S.A.

First Edition
First Printing, 2001

Book design and editing by Michael Maupin
Cover art © 2001 by Digital Stock and Photodisc
Cover design by Gavin Dayton Duffy

The names of some of the various witnesses appearing in this book have been changed, and pseudonyms were used to protect their privacy.

Library of Congress Cataloging-in-Publication Data
Dennett, Preston E., 1965–
    Extraterrestrial visitations : true accounts of contact /
    Preston Dennett. — 1st ed.
        p.   cm.
    Includes bibliographical references and index.
    ISBN 1-56718-220-8
        1. Human-alien encounters. 2. Alien abduction. I. Title.
    BF2050.D46 2001
    001.942—dc21

                                                        2001029249

Llewellyn Publications
A Division of Llewellyn Worldwide, Ltd.
P.O. Box 64383, Dept. 1-56718-220-8
St. Paul, MN 55164-0383, U.S.A.
www.llewellyn.com

Printed in the United States of America

Other Books by Preston Dennett

*UFO Healings: True Accounts of
People Healed by Extraterrestrials*
(Wild Flower Press, 1996)

One in Forty: The UFO Epidemic
(Kroshka Books, 1996)

UFOs Over Topanga Canyon
(Llewellyn Publications, 1999)

Contents

Introduction

The UFO phenomenon remains one of the most perplexing and persistent mysteries of modern times. Since pilot Kenneth Arnold sighted twelve flying disk-like objects over Mount Rainier, Washington, in June 1947, reports of UFO activity have escalated across the world. What started with simple sightings of metallic craft evolved into what appears to be direct face-to-face contact with extraterrestrial beings. There are many different facets of this phenomenon; however, it quickly becomes obvious that the central focus of alien visitation involves abduction or contact with humans.

Alien abductions can be defined as the closest of all UFO encounters, in which a person, or persons, are taken inside an extraterrestrial craft. In some cases the abduction is involuntary, much in the nature of a kidnapping. In other cases, the experience appears to be voluntary, in which people are invited aboard of their own free will.

What happens once someone is inside the craft varies greatly; however, there are patterns. According to several studies of onboard encounters, the so-called "examination" is the most common. This usually involves the abductee/experiencer being laid out on an examination table. A typical medical examination takes place, during which samples are taken of hair, skin, nails, saliva and, in some cases, reproductive materials such as sperm or ovum. Other experiences onboard include surgeries, mental and emotional testing, presentation of babies, prophetic revelations, and spiritual encounters.

In 1987, Thomas E. Bullard released the results of his pioneering statistical study of 309 abduction cases. His study was among the first to outline an ordered sequence of events to alien abductions. According to Bullard, there are eight main events that occur: *capture, examination, conference, tour, otherworldly journey, divine message, return,* and *aftermath.*

An example of a composite case might involve a man driving alone late at night when he sees an unidentifiable object sending down a blue beam of light, levitating him inside the object. He finds himself surrounded by five short humanoid creatures with large hairless heads, large dark eyes, and diminutive features. A medical examination takes place, samples are taken, and a brief explanation is given. The man is healed of a physical ailment. A close-up staring procedure takes place during which one alien seems to read the man's thoughts. He is given various tests measuring his emotional reactions. The abductee is then taken to see what appear to be alien-human hybrid babies. Afterwards he is taken to see perhaps the engine room, or some other part of the ship. Finally, he is taken to what appears to be another planet, perhaps another dimension, or he may have an out-of-body experience. He is then told prophecies of future events, warnings of environmental disaster to earth, and is given messages of a spiritual or theological nature. Afterward he is returned to his car with only the memory of the close-up UFO sighting. In the hours following the experience, he notices increased thirst, a strong desire to sleep, and a general feeling of anxiety. He may notice unusual marks or scars on his body. Later, he begins to have psychic premonitions, uncovers his memories of the experience, and begins to make major changes in his life. What he at first thought was a frightening, negative experience, he now feels was ultimately beneficial. It is important to note that virtually no cases have all these elements, but all have some.

Of course, onboard UFO encounters are as unique as the people who have them. Different researchers have come up with surprisingly different scenarios, perhaps dependent on the focus of their research. Some researchers feel that alien abductions are negative experiences, offering only physical and mental trauma, with little lasting benefit to the unfortunate victims. Other researchers feel that these contacts are positive experiences, offering those lucky enough to have them everything from improved health to spiritual enlightenment. Of course, there is every range in between.

Alien abductions also seem to be defined geographically. In the United States, abduction accounts are overwhelmingly dominated by reports of three-to-five-foot-tall beings with large dark eyes, oversized hairless heads, and whitish-gray skin. Many of the reports from South America involve dwarf-like beings, often hairy, with unusual, though vaguely human, features. In England and Europe, many accounts involve encounters with beings described very much like humans.

Of course, these are just generalizations. It is not clear whether these differences are due to cultural interpretations of the same phenomenon, or actual differences in the "species" of extraterrestrial reported. In fact, recent research shows an increasing amount of bleed-through, with Americans reporting more human-like aliens, and Europeans reporting the short beings, or "small grays."

In either case, the accounts follow the same patterns. It is also evident that UFO encounters are a worldwide phenomenon, with accounts from virtually every country in the world. Although the United States leads the world in terms of the number of abduction reports, hundreds of reports have come from Canada, South America, England, Africa, Australia, Europe, and Russia. All of these reports follow the same general events as outlined by Bullard, of being taken onboard, examined, and returned.

The actual number of reported abductions remains a matter of some controversy. Some researchers maintain that abductions are relatively rare events, while others claim that they may number in the millions. Others feel that they may be primarily psychological events and others take a more "nuts-and-bolts" interpretation, in which such experiences are primarily physical events.

I personally became involved in UFO research in 1986 when a series of events led me to start an investigation into the subject of UFOs. I had always regarded UFOs as the product of fantasy. Then, one evening in November 1986, I heard a report on the evening news of a UFO sighting over Alaska. I didn't believe it for a second, but I made the mistake of asking my friends, family, and coworkers what they thought of it. One by one, they came forward and told me that not only did they believe the report, but they, too, had had a UFO encounter!

Some people of course laughed, but not everyone. My brother related that he and two friends saw a UFO, and chased it in their car for several miles. My sister-in-law described her own terrifying face-to-face encounter with gray-type aliens. Two coworkers described missing-time encounters with UFOs, and several friends told me of their own very close encounters with metallic disks.

Needless to say, I was shocked. I had not been taught about the phenomenon in school. When the reports were mentioned in the media, it was always very tongue-in-cheek. And most shocking, the people who had just revealed their encounters to me were all people I trusted implicitly. I knew they were not lying. They explained their previous silence on the subject as due to fear of others' disbelief and ridicule. Many had mentioned their encounters earlier, only to be met with hostile reactions from the people they loved. They therefore learned to "just keep quiet."

The realization that these unknown craft were abducting people I knew caused a radical shift in my worldview. I quickly devoured every book on the subject and then moved out of the armchair and into the field, where I began interviewing witnesses and conducting onsite investigations. Since then, I have interviewed hundreds of witnesses and investigated cases of virtually every type. I have joined every UFO group I could find. I have written more than seventy articles and three books (*One in Forty: The UFO Epidemic, True Accounts of Close Encounters with UFOs*, 1996; *UFO Healings: True Accounts of People*

Healed by Extraterrestrials, 1996; and *UFOs Over Topanga Canyon,* 1999) I went on the radio and on television, and began speaking at meetings and conventions. I gave my name to the local police, who referred to me several cases. I began traveling to UFO sighting hotspots and attempting to make contact myself. In a matter of a few years, UFOs had completely taken over my life. Today I continue to do active UFO research, and have focused much of my efforts on trying to educate people about the phenomenon.

This book contains some of the most extensive and intense cases I have ever investigated. UFO sightings are, by themselves, very interesting. However, often there is little interaction between the witnesses and the object observed. I have tried to limit the cases in this book to those involving considerable interaction between the witnesses and the experiences they encountered. In most cases this involves either an onboard encounter, or a face-to-face encounter with extraterrestrial beings.

I have often been asked whether or not extraterrestrials are friendly or hostile. This question is not as easy to answer as one might assume. Many witnesses experience extreme fear during their encounters, despite the fact that they are not harmed in any way. Some abductees feel extremely violated, while others feel truly blessed. Some appear to have genuinely negative experiences, while others appear to have genuinely positive experiences.

Again, it seems that UFO encounters are as individual as the people who have them. Sometimes it seems that how a person reacts emotionally during an encounter can have a profound effect on how they interpret the experience. How they react physically seems to affect how they are actually treated. Understandably, someone who reacts with fear and outrage may be deemed dangerous and therefore physically restrained by the extraterrestrials. Someone who reacts calmly may be given greater liberties of movement. Someone overcome with fear may not be able to observe or communicate as easily as someone who remains calm and composed.

I have always felt that the persons most qualified to speak on the subject of extraterrestrial contact are the people who have had the experiences. In this book you will find both men and women who have had profound contact with extraterrestrials. Each account is told in the witnesses' own words. Each witness reacted in their own unique way to their experience.

There is the case of a young man who saw an unidentifiable object along with hundreds of other witnesses. However, when he left the area, he was followed by a craft that eventually struck him with a beam of light, starting an ordeal that he would not forget.

There is the case of a woman who experienced a terrifying "missing-time" abduction as a child, only to be plagued by unusual experiences her whole life, culminating in a face-to-face encounter with extraterrestrials on a lonely mountain road in the middle of the night.

There is the case of a young woman who had an extremely close-up sighting with a metallic craft, which prompted childhood memories of a bizarre nighttime visitation of a strange entity in her bedroom.

There is the case of a young man who experienced a six-hour ordeal aboard a craft that abducted him in full view of his mother and brother.

The other cases are just as incredible. However, as incredible as they may appear, they are all absolutely true.

Sightings

The following accounts focus on cases in which people have had missing time encounters during which they've seen and interacted with extraterrestrial beings. However, it is important to note that there are many, many cases of simple UFO sightings. Each sighting adds another piece of evidence pointing to the reality of the phenomenon. Regular sightings are just as important to research. After all, *something* or *someone* is inside these things.

Many sighting cases are also related to abduction cases. In other words, one person's most amazing sighting of a UFO is sometimes another person's most terrifying alien abduction. For most people, however, a UFO sighting doesn't mean abduction is imminent. The most common UFO encounter is a simple and brief sighting of a star-like object high in the sky, unlike an aircraft, moving in an anomalous way.

Another problem about sightings: where does one draw the line between sighting and encounter? For example, what if someone has a sighting of a UFO that's very close, and yet there was no *apparent interaction* between the object and the witness? What if someone has a distant sighting of a UFO, but feels that there was also telepathic contact associated with the sighting? What about cases where the interaction is limited to the appearance of a UFO and the panic of a large crowd of people? Or what if the witness to a UFO sighting becomes *spiritually transformed* by the sighting? Every time one draws a line and categorizes the UFO contact experience, another case comes along and defies explanation. For these reasons, I've decided to include four cases that almost crossed the line from sighting to very close encounter. This will also serve as an introduction to very close encounters with extraterrestrials, without immediately diving into the deep end.

The first case occurred on March 16, 1994, in Granada Hills in southern California. This case is interesting because it had multiple witnesses, viewing objects very close up, and occurred in a location where it should've been noticed by dozens of people, and yet nobody seemed to notice.

Kelly works as an emergency medical technician. At the time of her sighting, she was an office clerk. It occurred while she drove through a densely populated suburb, right near a movie theater and several stores. There were other people walking on the sidewalk and several other cars on the street.

She first saw a group of lights hovering about a hundred feet high, that not only looked strange, but moved strangely. As she recalled, "I saw in the distance these three lights that looked odd to me. And I thought maybe they were helicopters. And the closer I got, it was really low. And it was red lights that were really long and they were blinking. I don't know. I got close to it and it just wasn't a helicopter, and it wasn't an airplane because it was going too slow. I know it wasn't an airplane. I know it wasn't a helicopter because I could see it. It was so low. I don't know if it was round, but it looked flat . . . but it looked round. It looked like it was round . . . it was big. And you know how when helicopters hover above whatever they're wanting, you know how they're low and they shine their lights? It was about that low. And no noise. You know how helicopters make noise? Nothing."

She did her best to maneuver her car and watch the object at the same time. She also didn't feel any fear. "It was really interesting. I wish it didn't go away. I wanted it to stay there. Because I was driving and I almost got into an accident. I opened up my sunroof so I could see straight up."

Kelly eventually stopped her car. At this point, the object was only a few hundred feet away. Nobody else around seemed to notice something that was very evident in the sky. Kelly did what anyone should do if they see a UFO—get more witnesses. Kelly said, "I got out when I parked it, and I walked over to these men that were standing outside of the store. And I said, 'You guys might think I'm really crazy, but look at this thing.' And I told them, and they said, 'I don't know what that is, but it's something.'"

Eventually the object moved off, leaving Kelly amazed and convinced of the UFO phenomenon. "Before I really didn't think of it at all, but now I definitely think of it."

The next sighting is interesting because of its location, right outside Nellis Air Force Base, also known as Area 51, where our government is allegedly reverse-engineering extraterrestrial craft. The next witness may have seen one of these craft.

Zoli Meszaros works as a custom car upholstery installer. On August 20, 1993, Zoli was driving on the highway leading west out of Las Vegas, Nevada. His mother sat in the right passenger seat. It was about 9:00 P.M. when Zoli noticed an unusual star-like light very low on the horizon, about four or five miles away. He recalled, "For about ten miles, I saw this little light.

I thought it was a star at first, some kind of bright light because it was still when I first saw it. Then it moved. It moved across the sky. It moved from the left side of the windshield, all the way across the sky to the right side of the windshield, the passenger side. It even went past the passenger side where I couldn't see it. Then it came back across the front of us again so that I saw it again. It was really fast. It was going up and down. It would go from left to right the whole length of the windshield. I don't know if you can figure that— I'd say a few miles in a matter of seconds. It wasn't like one of our aircraft. It went back and forth and up and down. It went from left to right, then it hesitated for a second, then went diagonal up, then straight down, then diagonal again, then across the sky again, and kind of hovered a little bit, and then it took off. It went back and forth a few times, then up and down. On the right side, it went up and down, and then a little bit diagonal, and it would shoot across the sky to the left side and do the same thing. It just kept repeating it."

Zoli and his mother were mesmerized and excited by what they saw. Zoli said to his mother, "Look at that! Look at that! Can you see it?! Can you see it?!"

She replied, "Yes!"

As it darted, Zoli said, "You see it going to the left? You see it going up and down?" Zoli's mother saw everything he saw. Zoli recalled, "My mom saw it. I made sure she saw what I was seeing. She saw it, clear as day. She saw the same thing I saw."

The object's appearance was really just a light, about as bright as a very bright star. Said Zoli, "It was just a white light. There were no blinking lights, no red lights. It was just one light. And I knew it wasn't a helicopter or an airplane because it was just moving too fast. It was pretty wild . . . It was really weird."

The movement was totally unconventional. The way the object turned at right angles, hovered perfectly still, and then darted across the sky—these maneuvers ruled out conventional aircraft. "It did it really rapidly." Zoli remembered. "It didn't do it like it was making a turn. It just did it. It was going backwards and forwards, and up and down at its will, just directly. It would go really quick. It didn't take time to circle and turn around and speed up. It just went left, right, up, down, then back left and all the way across right again . . . it was not any kind of fighter plane like an F-15, or an F-18. It was nothing like that, because I've seen those turn around, and they have to do a big swooping turn. And this thing was just going left, right, just *bam-bam-bam* . . . it was something that was far, far, far more advanced than I've seen that we have, that's public."

Zoli found out later that the sighting location was adjacent to Area 51. Still, he insists that he and his mother saw *something unusual.* "I'm not ignorant of anything like that. I know what I saw. And I know it wasn't any kind of light. And I know it wasn't a shooting star. And I know it wasn't any kind of airplane that we fly, or a helicopter even. Because this moved way too fast for any of that stuff. It was wild. . . . I've never seen anything like that. If I were to say anything, it was a UFO, unless the government has something high-tech like that. It was just moving way too fast and abrupt, and just precise turns, not turns but switching directions. It was incredible. Like I said, maybe the government has something that does that, that we don't know about. But other than that, I would assume it is a UFO."

After watching for five minutes, Zoli noticed the object darted away towards the northeast. He admits he was baffled by what he saw, but was it extraterrestrial or human? He's not sure.

The third case is interesting because it involves a close-up sighting of a solid metallic craft that appeared before a large crowd. Today Claudia Blacios works in a business office. In 1972, while in Paramount, in southern California, she and her family had a close-up UFO sighting that they will never forget. Claudia was then only five years old. She, her younger sister, and her mom and dad piled into the family's Volkswagen Beetle and headed off to the local drive-in movie theater. The parking lot was filled with people as the movie started. It had just started getting dark. Suddenly, a large, oval-shaped, metallic-silver object appeared right next to and above the movie screen. What happened next was incredible. The crowd panicked, dropping their popcorn and drinks as they made a mad dash for the exits and away from the object. As Claudia remembered, "They had turned on the film. My sister and I were messing around in the back. All of a sudden, we see people running past us, and cars honking, and headlights turning on and off. I don't know what's going on. I hear a lady scream-ing. And I finally asked my dad, 'Dad, what's going on?'

"And my dad said, 'Nothing.' So I remember peeking between the seats to look at my mom and dad to see why they were acting so weird, and why all those people were walking so fast to their cars and dropping their popcorn. I saw my dad's face and it was just completely frozen and just pale. And my mom's was the same.

"And all of a sudden, I look out the window and I see a strange thing. It wasn't a plane. It was . . . it was . . . it was kind of long like a cigar, but it was metallic. I remember I distinctly saw the color of it. It was metallic. I remember asking my father what that was. And I started tugging on my sister, 'Look, look, look!' . . . she looked.

"We're just staring at this thing, and people are fighting to exit, to go out the exits that are in the front and the back. And cars are honking and a lot of people are leaving. And my dad just sat there and didn't do anything. I was just looking at it. I even remember it had a light, but it didn't have colored lights . . . it was silver, silver like a spoon. . . . There were like windows. They didn't look like windows like on an airplane. They were going all the way across, but they weren't exactly square. And there was this one light, and it was on the bottom . . . and it was just making this weird sound. It sounded like a whir, but it was very, very low . . . like a little droning sound, but it was very, very faint, in between all the screaming.

"It was there for a while. It was kind of like watching us watch the movie, like wondering what are we watching. It was almost the size of the screen, but it was a lot thinner. It was oval. And it was just watching us watch the movie. And I thought that was really odd, because why would it want to watch what we're watching? . . . the thing hovered there for maybe five minutes . . . and then eventually it went straight up. I was trying to see it out the VW window, but I couldn't see it. It just went straight up. . . . I don't know how long it was there for . . . I didn't realize it was there until I saw my parents' faces just frozen, staring at it, and then everybody else started running.

"I remember my mom and dad never talked about it again. It was just one of those things you don't ever think about. It wasn't until about three years ago that I was listening to a radio station, and they were having a discussion on UFOs. And people were calling in with their stories and encounters. And this one gentleman called, and he was at the same drive-in theater at the same time, watching the same movie, and described the same thing. And that's when I looked at my mom and my mom looked at me and I said, 'We were there!'

"My mom said, 'Yeah, that was a long time ago.'

"And I said, 'Why didn't we ever talk about it?'

"'I don't know.' She said. 'We just never talked about it.' But we were there. And that guy was describing the events just as I remember them, with the ship being there, and people leaving."

It may seem strange that nobody discussed the UFO sighting, but as we shall see, this odd feature turns up in case after case. About her own encounter, Claudia recalled, "All through high school I always had this curiosity about that. Because in the back of my mind, I knew that I had seen one. I remember I would think about it, but not really dwell on it, not a lot. And it wasn't until I heard that gentleman [on the radio], and we finally discussed it."

The last case involves a man who had a close-up encounter with a UFO that changed his life. Before his encounter, David Perez was not a happy man. He was in his mid-twenties and had worked a number of low-paying jobs. However, various issues in his life, financial struggles, relationships, and health problems had caused him to become increasingly depressed and, at times, suicidal.

He then had a UFO encounter that had a huge impact on his life. He had seen strange darting lights on a few occasions, but his next encounter had a profound effect upon him. He was in his apartment in West Covina, California, in October 1997, a few weeks after the mass suicide in San Diego of forty-nine members of the so-called "Heaven's Gate" UFO cult.

David had just read some of the material related to the case and was amazed at the way the cult leader, Marshall Applewhite, had meshed together religious beliefs with the UFO phenomenon. At the time, David had had little exposure to UFO literature, and had no idea that there are dozens of cases on record in which UFO experiences and religious "miracles" are inextricably intertwined; that people actually report seeing religious figures during UFO encounters.

Immediately after reading, David went outside with his cousin to smoke a cigarette. David spotted the object first. As he recalled, "I happened to look up in the sky, and I saw this . . . uh . . . it looked like a ship. I knew right away it wasn't an airplane or a helicopter. It was really moving slow. I mean, we were watching it for ten minutes. And then it got kind of close [enough] for us to see more of the body. All I saw at first were the lights all the way around it. And I never saw lights like that around a helicopter or an airplane. There were two red lights in the middle, a blue one above that. And alongside the red ones were bright white ones. And below that were I think two yellow ones. And my cousin and I were just staring at it.

"All of a sudden, it stopped. And I saw a real bright light with—it looked like smoke coming through it. Picture a spotlight with somebody blowing smoke through it. It looked just like that. And then it started going real, real slow again for maybe another twenty feet, and it stopped. And then that light came on again. And then it took off for another twenty feet, and then that light happened again. It did that light maybe five or six times."

David and his cousin continued watching the object. Not only was it moving strangely, but it looked strange, sending down a powerful beam of light. The beam was unusual in that it was opaque, and extremely bright.

David's girlfriend also came out and saw the object. She quickly became frightened and went back inside.

While David and a few others observed the object, a neighbor came out and started screaming, "The sky is falling! What is this idiot looking at?!"

David felt extremely angry with the neighbor. He was just about to lose his temper when something very unusual happened. "I was just about to tell her something. She had finally gotten on my nerves. And then, all of a sudden, in the middle of these lights, this red bright light went on, and it seemed like it kind of penetrated my pupils, and my vision turned red. Everything that I saw was tinted red. . . . That's when I got kind of scared. I thought it had screwed up my vision. And I wasn't able to cuss her out like I wanted to . . . I wanted to cuss her back, but I just couldn't talk, and I couldn't move or anything. I don't know if it was the fear or what, but I just couldn't move or anything.

"But then, all of a sudden, that light went off, and my vision slowly went back to normal."

David was shocked not only because he was apparently "zapped" by the object, but because of his reaction to it. He stumbled back inside without even looking back at it. A few minutes later, his cousin came in, and they discussed what they saw. Somehow, the discussion turned into an argument, and David ended up driving away, only to have another encounter with the same object. David remembered, "I took off in the car, and I got on the freeway, and I ended up all the way in Canoga Park. I got off the freeway, and I got back on the freeway coming in the other direction. I swear, people were coming inches away from my car going, like, eighty or ninety miles an hour. And I got really scared because I thought I was going to die . . . they were coming so close to my car, so close, cutting me off. They were going crazy. I was getting scared, and then I started getting mad. I started getting so mad that I hit my dashboard. I felt like I was going to snap. And all of a sudden, I felt really, really warm and comforted. I mean, my fear just totally went away. And I looked out the window, and by the moon I saw that ship that was over here in West Covina . . . I felt comforted all the sudden, and I looked up and there was that ship . . . But it was kind of close. I think that was the closest I saw it. And I just felt really comforted. I really did."

Again, David's emotions did a complete turnaround as a direct result of his encounter with the UFO. David drove home calmly. When he parked and got out, he looked up and, amazingly, there was the same object. It had apparently followed him. "I looked up and sure enough I saw that ship. And when it took off, I felt like . . . I guess the best I can put it is, relieved."

David was not only emotionally affected by the UFO, but *physically* affected too. "I was kind of stressed." He said. "I've always had problems with my back. I used to cough up blood once in a while. I was kind of sick. I had pains in my chest and on my side. Ever since that night, I haven't had any pain at all. And I was also suicidal, and ever since that night, I haven't been. I've been good. I've been feeling really good, really healthy."

David is certain the UFO somehow healed him, but he has no idea how. He just knows that the encounter changed him. The last profound reaction was to reaffirm his belief in spirituality and God. "I kind of feel for some strange reason that they have something to do with God," he related. "Ever since then I've started talking about God."

He started experiencing premonitions and developed a sudden interest in meditation and psychic development. Although his encounter remains unexplained, he feels it had a positive effect on his life. David's encounter is interesting because although he never came face-to-face with extraterrestrials, and although he could account for no missing time, there was an interaction between him and the UFO that went beyond a mere sighting, probably occurring when he was "zapped" by a red light from the object.

These sighting accounts help set the stage for the remarkable encounters to follow.

"None of Us Talked About It"

One hot summer evening in 1962, sixteen-year-old Rob Baldwin and three of his friends were looking for something to do in their farming community outside Ann Arbor, Michigan. The rural area had its benefits: clean air, natural beauty, and virtually no crime; however, for a teenager, it was just a place to exercise one's boredom.

This particular evening was no different. Sometimes they would drive around, looking for something to do, or just talk. On this occasion Rob and his friends piled into his 1955 Ford stick-shift and drove off. They had recently heard that UFOs were being sighted around the area, and they jokingly thought

they would get out of town and see if there was anything to it.

They ended up along Denton Road, popularly
known as "the Farmer's Lane," a narrow, straight dirt
road in the middle of farming country. The landscape
was mostly flat with occasional rolling hills. Denton
road was lined with full-grown elm trees canopying
the road, providing shade and a windbreak. They kept
driving until they reached a dip in the road about five
or six feet deep and a few car-lengths long. Parking
alongside the road in the center of the depression,
which would hide them from any vehicles coming
from either direction, they rolled down the windows,
and began talking about whatever came to their
minds. The night was very warm. The crickets chirped
merrily and the frogs croaked loudly. They had only
been parked for about twenty minutes; it was just past
midnight.

Suddenly, the four young men were confronted
with an extremely unusual sight. Just ahead of them,
on the road, a very large, glowing, egg-shaped object
appeared just over the lip of the culvert. It hovered
perfectly still, stopping its forward movement the
instant it came into sight of the witnesses.

Rob Baldwin describes what happened in his own
words. "This craft—the only thing I could figure out is
that it was basically following the road, hovering over
the road, maybe three or four feet above the road. It

came straight down the center of the road. From one part of the depression, the dip, to the other part of the dip was probably fifty feet, and we were parked somewhere in the middle of it. So this craft is coming down the center of the road, and when it got to the top of the depression where we were parked, and as soon as it—I would imagine—saw us, and we saw it probably about the same time, it stopped and hovered basically on the edge of the drop down into the gully or the depression that we were in. And it just stopped and we looked at it. And I'm sure it was observing us."

At this point, all conversation stopped cold. The boys looked at each other and back at the huge egg-shaped object that was hovering mere feet away. They wondered what would happen next.

At first, nothing happened. The occupants of both vehicles were evidently caught by surprise, and each was, for the moment, staying perfectly still and observing each other. The teenagers were completely awestruck.

Rob recalled, "It was shaped like a giant egg, and basically the same proportions, only very large. It was probably eight feet in diameter and ten feet high. And one of the interesting things about it was the coloration. It was everything from crimson-red to yellow-gold. And the colors seemed to flow around, basically defining the surface of the craft, and just flowed over and around the craft simultaneously. It was just like a giant infusion of colors . . . everything from crimson red, and orange and yellow were there. It was incredibly beautiful. And we were just mesmerized by this thing, watching the colors flow around it.

"And at [the] same time, it was emitting some type of white gas, kind of like a gas or a smoke or something, maybe something like the gas you would see off of dry ice as it was dissolving. And it was completely silent. We never heard a thing. And for a period of time, we observed it. I'm not really sure how long we looked at it, thinking back on it. It was at least fifteen seconds to a half a minute that we watched it. It could have been two or three minutes, I'm not really sure."

The four young men could hardly believe their eyes. The object hovered steadily less than fifty feet away. It was about the size of a small room, shaped almost exactly like an egg, sitting upright, with the large side on the bottom. Bright swirling colors covered its surface and white mist enveloped the object. It hung just beneath the thick canopy of the trees, lighting up the whole area with vivid shades of red, orange, and yellow. To Rob, it was one of the most beautiful things he had ever seen.

For an undetermined period of time, the face-off between humans and extraterrestrials continued. Eventually, however, Rob's curiosity overcame his fear and he decided to make a move. Rob said, "We were all blown away by it. The first thing we thought was, 'What in the hell is that?' I'm sure we were thinking,

'Is this swamp gas? I don't think so!' It stayed totally stationary. It just glided towards us and stopped. It was totally stationary, no wobble, no movement, just the colors flowing around it. It was caught underneath the canopy of the trees, hovering over the road. It was no further than fifty feet away. We were just sitting there, and we were all just blown away by this incredibly beautiful craft, or whatever it was. I mean, this thing was incredible."

"And finally," Rob continued, "I decided that I would go towards it. . . . I didn't get out of the car and try to embrace it. I wanted to maintain the distance between me and the craft. I think more than anything it was kind of a bravado thing that provoked me to drive towards the vehicle. And I started the car up. I left the lights out and I started moving slowly towards it. And as I moved towards it, it maintained the distance and backed off, and went over the hill out of our sightline.

"And when it started going over the hill, I floored it, right at it, you know, a typical teenage thing. And by the time I got to the top of the hill which was, you know, a second or two, this thing was just like an orange blur going down the road. You could just see this orange streak. And it had found a hole in the canopy and shot up through the canopy and was out of sight in like three, four, maybe five seconds. It never made a sound. And it traveled at an incredible rate of speed. From the start of the acceleration on, it was amazing. . . . On this particular farmer's road, elm trees lined the side of the field as windbreaks and snowbreaks. And they completely canopied the road for about a half, three-quarters, maybe a mile. And by the time I got to the top of the hill, this thing was just breaking through a hole in the canopy and it had already gone a mile or whatever the distance was. I had floored it and I was chasing it when it disappeared into the heavens. It vanished into a dot. I mean, it was going almost as fast as a meteor goes in the sky."

The four teenagers were utterly amazed by their encounter. It was the most unusual thing they had ever seen. They had heard UFOs were in the area; however, many people were saying it was "just swamp gas." After their encounter, they knew that *swamp gas* was definitely *not* what they had seen. What they saw could only have been a *craft*. The way it flew—hovering perfectly still, and then shooting out of sight in mere seconds—they all knew that it was nothing built by humans. They never saw windows or markings of any kind. They never felt any physical sensations nor heard any noise whatsoever. The object just appeared over the edge of the dip and after a few moments, then took off at top speed.

The story gets even stranger. One would think that after an event such as a UFO sighting, the witnesses would be eager to discuss what they had just encountered. In fact, just the opposite happened. For some inexplicable reason, the subject was taboo. It was as if nothing unusual had even happened. "One of the strange things about it," Robb recalled, "was I don't remember talking about it after that. I mean, I don't remember talking about it at all. In fact, I don't remember anything about that night at all, after that experience. . . . Basically, the event was just warehoused for twenty, twenty-five years. Pretty strange. I don't remember anything. Nothing at all."

It wasn't until years later that Rob realized the experience's aftereffects were nearly as inexplicable as the event itself. Unknown to Rob at the time, however, is that his reaction is actually typical of people who have just had a "missing-time" experience with a UFO. Almost as if they are hypnotized, people who are taken aboard a UFO are often left with no memory of the onboard segment of the experience, then afterwards, little or no discussion is made about the experience.

In the years following the experience, Rob had talked to other people who also had close-up encounters, and only then did he realize that the aftereffects of the experience were not unique, and that there was a possibility of missing time and an onboard UFO abduction. "In retrospect," he said, "after talking to a number of people who have had experiences, that's fairly common, where for some reason you don't talk about it, even with the people that experienced it with you. So it's quite possible if I've had contact, that was the one time I've had contact."

As time went on, Rob realized more and more that his encounter was not only unexplained, but could possibly have been more than just a simple sighting. He became increasingly eager to locate his former childhood friends and discuss the experience with them. He had long since moved to California, but then came the opportunity he had been waiting for—a high-school reunion.

When the time came, he packed his bags and headed back to Michigan. His goal was to locate the other witnesses and discuss the incident in order to find out what they remembered about that one mysterious summer night. He expected to get pretty straightforward answers that would confirm his own memories. He was not at all prepared for the answers he received. He did get confirmation of the sighting; however, the other witnesses remembered things just a little differently.

The fact that bothered him the most about their encounter was he didn't remember anything that happened afterward. His friends' answers gave him even more reason for concern. Rob reported, "I have been wanting to talk to these guys about it. And finally, during my thirty-year reunion, I corralled them one at a time and asked them about it. And one of them didn't remember it at all! One of them told me a totally different story than what I had thought it was, and another one told me a different story with some additional information that I hadn't thought of, nor have I included in my story. What I told you now is the way I saw it. The story has never changed for me. I've never had any additions or subtractions or deletions or changes. That's the way it's always been for me.

"But one [of the guys] remembered it totally differently. He said it was somebody playing a joke on us. And they jumped out of the side of the road and they did something. And I just basically threw his interpretation completely out because I knew for sure it wasn't that. I think he was just making it up. I don't think he really recalled it. But the other fellow did. The way one of the other participants saw it was that we got out of the car and walked over to the farmer's field, which was just thirty, forty feet away from us, and then the craft hovered over us. He doesn't remember anything after that."

Rob was stunned. What did this mean? He always assumed his memory of the event was complete, except, of course, for afterward. But hadn't he seen the object move away? And the fact that one of the witnesses remembered it as a practical joke and the other had no memory of the event whatsoever—that seemed impossible. But it was the other man's memory of getting out of the car and having the object hover straight overhead that really shook him up. It was all extremely confusing. As Rob said, "What's amazing was that we had these different perceptions about this thing that was fairly straightforward in my impression. But obviously it wasn't."

What actually happened to the four teenagers that night? It's hard to say for sure, but there is every indication that there is more to the experience than they all remember. One obvious red flag pointing to missing time is the confusion about the period of time they observed the object. As Rob reported, they lost all sense of time as they observed it. However, he has no memory of ever leaving his car. On the other hand, he has no reason to doubt the memory of his other friend.

This apparent contradiction is actually a consistent feature of alien abductions. It's as if each participant is left with varying degrees of recall of the event. For one witness, his memory of the event was wiped completely clean. For another, it appeared as if a "screen memory" was placed over the event, causing him to think that it was all just a practical joke. Rob and his friend each remembered varying portions of the experience.

What probably happened should be fairly obvious. As the boys sat in their car, they were hidden from view. The object was apparently surprised to find them there, and both watched each other for a few moments. At this point, a probable abduction occurred. The boys were likely led out of their car into the nearby field, where they were taken aboard the craft. What happened aboard remains a mystery, however, they were apparently placed back into their vehicle after an undetermined period of time, at which point, Rob decided to give chase to the object. Only then did the object zoom away at high speed.

This scenario neatly accounts for the apparent contradiction of the witnesses' memories. The fact that they didn't discuss the incident afterwards is also strongly indicative of an extensive onboard UFO encounter. These are all details that turn up again and again following an alien abduction: screen memories, partial memories, differing memories, and the total absence of conversation following the experience.

Rob is quite aware that he is a possible abductee. Unlike many abductees, however, he has shied away from hypnosis. It's not that he doesn't trust hypnosis. He feels that someday he may allow himself to be hypnotized to gain a fuller recall of that night. But for now, he is content with his memories.

Since that night, Rob has become increasingly interested in the UFO phenomenon. He has read a number of books, talked to a number of UFO witnesses, and eventually formed a UFO group that meets monthly to listen to lectures by leading UFO researchers. He has also had a number of other sightings. Once, while in Sedona, Arizona, he saw three golden disks moving across the sky. What was strange about this experience, however, was that there was a helicopter directly in front of the disks, and another one directly behind, as if the objects were being escorted by our own military. On another occasion, while driving along a freeway in southern California, he saw a metallic craft complete with portholes hovering very high in the daylight sky.

Rob has no idea why he has had so many UFO encounters. However, he does admit that the answers may be found in some very odd experiences he had as a toddler. "I think," he said, "I might have had some experiences with that kind of stuff when I was a kid. I had some strange stuff happen in my bedroom, like not being able to move and being awake, that kind of stuff."

Not being able to move upon awakening can be caused by a condition known as "sleep paralysis" or "night terror." This often occurs during a lucid dream, when the dreamer is aware that he or she is dreaming. The paralysis prevents people from acting out their dreams during sleep, something that could be dangerous. Many skeptics have pointed to this condition in an attempt to explain the entire abduction scenario. This, of course, comes nowhere near explaining alien abductions.

It can be confusing because the phenomenon of waking up paralyzed is also a common feature of alien abductions. Often abductees will wake up unable to move and then find themselves confronted with extraterrestrial entities. Rob Baldwin probably falls under this latter category. As he recalled, "[I had] some scary stuff moving around in my bedroom, that I thought was scary. It was something that wouldn't let me see it. I couldn't quite ever get my eyes turned over to see it. Because my head was frozen and they were always on the side of me."

To any UFO researcher, the above account will sound very familiar. Although Rob doesn't recall actually seeing anything, he was all too aware of something present in the room with him. Although he doesn't recall any other details, he remembers the events vividly. But he prefers not to make too much fuss about what happened. For him, it's all just a part of life's experience.

The Bony Crab Monster

Laura Caigoy never gave much thought to the idea of extraterrestrials or UFOs. That is, at least not until she had a close-up encounter with a metallic craft that hovered over her street one spring night in 1966.

At the time, Laura was in her last year of high school and lived in a densely populated suburb of Cicero, Illinois. Her life was typical of most teenagers. She spent her time doing schoolwork, thinking about boys, and exploring the bustling neighborhood around her home. Her weekends were usually spent visiting with her best friend, Ruthie.

This particular weekend was no different. She had spent all of Saturday, and most of Sunday, with Ruthie, watching television, listening to Ruthie's father's police scanner, or just talking. Unfortunately, it was a school night and she had to return home. She called her mother to pick her up and went outside with Ruthie to wait. As they climbed into Ruthie's parents' station wagon, so began one of the strangest events in their young lives.

Laura recalled, "We got bored waiting in the house, so we went to her dad's old station wagon. She got in the back seat and laid with her back facing me. And I got in the front seat and I laid across the seat next to the steering wheel and stuck my feet out in the window. And we weren't tired or anything. We were wide awake. And we had just been laughing. We were very much awake—laughing and chattering away. I even remember what we were talking about. We were talking about a band we liked. We just finished laughing, and I heard—more felt than heard—this something. It was in my ears. And I said, 'What is that?'

"And she didn't answer. I thought she was just waiting to listen to it, and she didn't answer at all. And I said it again, and nothing. I pulled my feet back in the car and got out. And I looked to the right and I could see Cermack Road, which is a really big street. I could see traffic and all that, and nothing but dark sky and trees and things like that. I didn't see a thing. So I looked to the left and nothing there either. And it was getting louder and I could feel it even more. . . .

When I turned to look back towards the right, there I saw it.

"It was a saucer coming on a slight angle down the street. And it was just there. It wasn't there a second ago. As much time as it takes you to turn your head is how fast it was there. And it was getting really close. I just couldn't imagine how it could have gotten there without me seeing it come from a distance. Because it was dark; you would have seen it. . . . I could see it coming in on a slight downward angle, straight down the block, a saucer too large to land in the street. It could only come down as far as the treetops and streetlamps would allow. I could not perceive any glint of metal—its surface appeared to be darker than the night sky.

"It was all lit up inside. It was totally illuminated inside with a yellow-white light. It was revolving slowly in a clockwise direction and had windows all the way around separated by struts except for one section. I could see right through the windows out the other side. The interior was a light color. I could make out its outline clearly. I always say it looked like an Oreo because of its silhouette. It was sort of convex on top, saucer-shaped, but not too rounded. And it was darker than the sky on the outside. . . . And the sky, it was really dark, it was just dark blue and I didn't see a moon. And the streetlights didn't shine on it at all because it was above them. And it just kept coming in.

It kept coming down the street, but it was too big to land in the street. I'm not really good at judging sizes, but it couldn't have landed in the street. It was wider than the street. I don't even think it could have landed on the sidewalk part. And it was revolving very slowly.

"As it came closer, it began to sound more like an engine on really, really slow idle. And the pulsing was even louder now. It was even more—I mean, I could feel it in my ears, you know, harder. And while this was happening—it was happening fairly fast—I was trying to get Ruthie to get up. And nothing. She would not respond, and just lay there. I bumped the car with my hip. I was real excited, so I was like slightly hysterical. It was pretty exciting. I mean, if it had been a plane and it was coming in for a crash, it would have been just as exciting.

"And there was nobody coming down the street. There was no traffic at all. And I just watched it kind of come over me. I didn't see anything under it. It was just dark, just black. And I couldn't see anything inside except this light. It was just totally illuminated. I didn't see any instruments or anything, or people. But you could see through the windows and out through the other side.

"And it was going so slowly. It was going so steady. I was just so amazed how it never wobbled or anything. It never wobbled or wavered in its course. I didn't see any props and there weren't any balloons or anything.

I thought it would have at least a prop, but nothing. And it just continued to come down the street. As it came closer to where I stood, it sounded like a very slow idling engine. It was only a few yards from where I stood, and again I tried to get Ruthie to witness this event. I called her name, 'Ruthie! Get out here! You have to see this!' Nothing! This was just not possible. Ruthie was a very light sleeper and she would not have fallen asleep while we were talking and laughing. By this time, it is directly over me. And as it got over me, I started to follow it."

Laura could hardly believe what was happening. She gave up trying to awaken Ruthie, and decided to just follow her instincts and see what would happen. She recalled, "I was real excited. I was happy. It was incredible. I mean, I couldn't believe it, because it was so low. I mean, if I had jumped up, I could have touched it. It was just above the streetlamps.

"I didn't see anything special happening underneath it, so I just dropped back a little so I could see into it some more. And as I got to about the middle of the block, there were three people. There were two old ladies. They were like a mother and daughter, but they were elderly, you know . . . with blue hair and house dresses. I didn't know them. I think I had seen them, but I didn't know them.

"And the other one, I guess it was a woman," Laura laughed. "It was Cicero. This was Cicero, and it was full of 'greasers.' They wear a lot of black. They have their hair slicked back a lot of times, and they wear sunglasses. That's why I wasn't so surprised to see this person wearing wraparound sunglasses at night. And her — I guess it was a her because she was small — her hair was waxed, slicked back, so it was very shiny. And she had her arms crossed, and her arms were sort of muscular. She had a white sleeveless shirt and black pants. She just stood there with her arms crossed and stared at me. And they never said a word. They just kind of looked at me. I said, 'Well, isn't this exciting?' And nothing, zip. And then they just looked back at the ship. They were watching it. And they saw me. . . . I was just walking down the middle of the street, and they're on the sidewalk. They were just standing there. They just turned to look at me, and then they looked back at the ship. And I followed it more until I couldn't follow it anymore because there was another street intersecting, another residential street.

"So I just watched it as long as I could. I started walking backwards so I could still see into it. . . . it was so leisurely. I just strolled. I had to slow up so I could look at it, so I could see in the windows. . . . And I never saw anything but the yellow white lights. I just like dropped back so that I could keep watching it. It just disappeared over the housetops. It didn't zoom away or disappear or anything. It [moved] just straight, just totally straight. It never veered in any way. It was just rock steady, and it was so incredible."

Laura had walked as far as she could, to where the street came to a T-intersection. She watched with a mixture of awe and disappointment as the craft moved slowly over the roofs of the houses that lined the next block. It was all she could do to keep herself from running up and knocking on her neighbor's doors and asking them if she could run through their home and into their backyard. Instead, she just stood there and watched the craft move slowly away.

She estimated that she had observed the craft for about five or ten minutes. However, when questioned, she admits that she might have lost track of time. "If there was any missing time, I couldn't have even known, because my watch was full of dried flowers. I didn't have any watch-works in there. I didn't know what time it was."

After the craft moved away over the housetops, Laura turned around and walked back up the street. Interestingly, even though only a few minutes had apparently passed, the other witnesses were nowhere to be seen. Laura related, "I turned and headed back to the car. By that time, those people were gone. And it was just like a minute. It's not a really big street, it's just a residential block. They were gone. And I got back to the car. Ruthie is still in the same position. And I

just knew this would happen, that's why I said in a normal voice, 'Ruthie?' And she was up like a shot. I mean,
she was just like *zoom!*, and was out of the car.

"I told her what happened. I excitedly relayed what
had transpired during her 'nap.' She was furious,
angry, and sputtering. She was really pissed because
she missed it. She ran into the house all sputtering
and got her parents, and they came running out. And
they said, 'Why didn't you call us?'

"'I didn't want to miss anything.' Because if I left
the street, it would have been gone."

Laura was flushed with excitement and awe. She
could hardly believe what had just happened, but neither could she deny it. The image of the craft hovering
less than thirty feet above her head was something she
would never forget.

Eventually, her mother arrived to take her home.
On the way back, Laura related her whole story. To her
disappointment, however, her mother didn't believe
her. Laura knew, however, that she had just had a very
unusual experience.

In fact, the more she reflected upon it, the more she
realized that *everything* about the experience was
unusual. First, the craft simply appeared overhead with
no warning. It made a very unusual noise that was *felt*
more than actually *heard*. It also looked very unusual.
Certainly, it was no conventional aircraft, and the fact

that Laura was so close, less than thirty feet, removes virtually any possibility of misperception.

But that's not all. One detail that Laura found exceedingly strange was the fact that her friend, Ruthie, fell asleep and would not wake up. One second they were talking and laughing, the next second Ruthie appeared to be in a deep sleep. As Laura recalled, "I don't know why she was out, I don't understand that. I really could have used a witness."

Laura had no way of knowing at the time that this is a common feature of very close encounters. Often one witness has a very close-up encounter, while others in the same area are put into some sort of trance state and remember absolutely nothing of the event. As improbable or amazing as it sounds, this detail turns up again and again in UFO accounts. After awhile, it becomes obvious that the UFO occupants are placing some of the witnesses into a state of unconsciousness while leaving others to experience the encounter.

Another very strange detail was the fact that there was no traffic on the street. "There should have been at least one or two cars." Laura said. "It was a popular street. It wasn't that far from Cermack. It's the biggest street in Cicero."

This again is another bizarre detail that turns up again and again. A UFO will appear over what should be a street busy with traffic, and yet no cars can be found. It's as if the UFO occupants are very much in control of the situation. In fact, it seems likely that the encounter was planned. The UFO occupants *knew* Laura was seeing them. They wanted her to see them. This encounter was *meant* for her.

There are also other indications that this was more than just a simple sighting. Besides the fact that Ruthie was "put to sleep" and traffic seemed to be diverted, there was also the question of the other witnesses. Laura did see other witnesses and they appeared to be looking at the craft, but then again, they weren't reacting in at all the way one would think someone would react upon seeing an unidentified flying object. They stood perfectly still, and betrayed no hint of excitement or awe. As Laura reacted, "I'm just surprised they didn't say anything."

What was even more strange was the bizarre appearance of one of the witnesses, the woman with the black hair and sunglasses. Laura was so impressed by her strange appearance that she remembered her in great detail. When asked again if the woman had an unusual appearance, Laura replied, "Did she? Well, yeah! She was really odd-looking for a woman. . . . [She wore] wraparound sunglasses. At that time I didn't really think much of it, because as I told you, Cicero is full of 'greasers,' and they would wear sunglasses at school, but only during the day. She was short. She had real smooth skin and her hair was totally slicked back, almost like it was painted on."

We have already discovered that screen memories often occur during encounters. Laura's description of this particular figure could be much more than it seems. The short stature, the smooth skin, the hair that looked "painted on," and particular the black wrap-around sunglasses—all these details sound very much like the description of a typical "small gray" alien. Also bizarre was the woman's unenthusiastic response to the sight of the craft. In fact, Laura remarked that it seemed the woman was just as interested in Laura as in the object!

After the encounter, Laura noticed no unusual physical symptoms. She had no unusual feelings, no unexplained scars, no bizarre flashbacks or strange dreams. Despite the fact that she felt all alone with her experience, Laura had no doubt in her mind that her encounter was absolutely real. It was so close to her.

And yet, she longed for some corroboration. Like many witnesses, she made a point to watch the news in the days that followed. Like most witnesses, she was to be sorely disappointed. She recalled, "I looked through the newspapers and listened to the radio and all that to see if anything had been reported. I watched for anything at all on TV, radio, and newspapers, but I never saw a thing. Nobody said anything. I was really surprised because it was hard to miss. I mean, you could not have missed it if you had been on the street. There would be no way."

So ended Laura's encounter. The sighting in no way frightened her. In fact, she felt extremely lucky to have seen something like that so close. For her, it was a very positive experience. At the time, she thought it was a "once-in-a-lifetime" event. However, as an adult, her son began reporting bizarre experiences. It wasn't long before she suddenly recalled some bizarre experiences from her own childhood. Slowly, she began to realize that her story was much more complicated than she originally thought.

It all began again about twenty-five years later. She and her family had moved to southern California, into a very old apartment built in 1912. It was her son that first started to complain about having unusual experiences. At first they thought it was just the apartment, and considered the possibility that it was haunted. But slowly, they realized that the explanation was probably something else entirely. Laura said, "I also suspect that my fifteen-year-old son is involved. My son is here. We used to live on Lafayette Park in L.A., and he was really freaked out about this one apartment we had. It was this really old building, like 1912, so it was basically an old house that had been chopped up into several apartments. The bathroom had a chimney going through it. And he was really scared of the chimney. He's not positive, but there was this thing that he called 'the bony crab monster.' It was like a torso with a skull head, and it was spider-like almost, and it had crab legs. And it took a piece of skin off his finger and said, 'Don't be afraid.' It said not to be afraid.

"I remember him telling me about that, and I didn't think anything of it. And these other things that he saw, they had like weasel-faces. They had long faces and trench coats. And they were all monochromatic—they were all a weird color, a tan. They were all one color. And he was really afraid of those. And I remember him telling me about it since he was four years old. They had big black, staring eyes. And I thought they were just dreams. I didn't even buy a UFO magazine. I wasn't even interested. We never heard about any of this stuff, so nobody influenced him. And I forgot all about it.

"And then we moved maybe a couple of years later. And he would have these weird dreams. He would wake up crying. Oh, they'd freak him out, and I really wasn't paying that much attention. I thought he was just having anxiety dreams, but I didn't know why."

Laura's son declined to talk to me directly, because, as Laura mentioned, "He doesn't like any of this." However, he did allow Laura to relay what he said. When she asked him if his dreams concerned "those creatures," he replied affirmatively. Laura related, "Those same creatures were in his dreams, just the weasel-faced things. We had a back door in our bedroom, and at one point he remembers floating through the backyard and seeing one of those weasel-faced things. And then at some point, he was having a lot of nosebleeds. And then I started having them for a few months and then they stopped. And that's all. I mean, I don't know if that's anything. I just thought it was weird with those weasel-faced things coming up again."

This account is riddled with red-flag indicators for UFO researchers. The description of the bony crab monsters and the weasel-faced creatures match very closely with other people's descriptions of extraterrestrials. The crab-like legs, the skinny torso, the skull-like head, and especially the large dark staring eyes—all are highly typical of the gray-type alien. Then there is also the report that they moved through a solid wall, and even took Laura's son with them—very much like a typical abduction account. But the most convincing detail is that Laura's son says that the aliens told him, "Don't be afraid." In account after account, this is the first message given to abductees by the extraterrestrials.

There are also the physical symptoms, including the fact that Laura's son was cut on his finger by one of the beings, and also that they both suffered from a series of nosebleeds during the period of Laura's son's "dreams."

The description of the aliens wearing trench coats may sound odd, however, even this bizarre detail occasionally turns up. It seems that Laura and her family are much more involved with the UFO phenomenon than they previously realized. Further evidence of this comes with Laura's own childhood memories. When she was a young child, something so outlandish occurred to her that she just filed it in the back of her mind and tried to forget about it. It not only seemed to make no sense, but it also scared her. As time went on, as she realized more and more that UFOs were becoming a part of her life, this one memory kept coming back. Finally, it got to the point where she could no longer ignore it.

As she related the memory, Laura actually apologized for its bizarreness. It seemed to her that it was too strange to have happened. She had no way of knowing that her story matched up with the reports of other abductees.

Laura remembered it keenly. "I was really, really young. I don't remember how old I was exactly, but it was about five. I just remember it didn't feel like a dream at all. And I wasn't sick, so I wasn't having one of those fever-things. I just remember feeling like there was this person next to me who looked like the joker on a deck of cards. I mean, he was white—a white face—and had this really big toothy smile. I don't remember what his nose looked like. His eyes were kind of squinty—you know—like the joker on the cards. And he had on the whole outfit. It was velvety, and it was purple and gold. And he was bouncing up and down and making this really weird noise. He looked like he was having a good time. He looked happy. And every time he bounced, I would hear this jingling. A harlequin outfit usually has bells on it, but I noticed this one didn't have bells on it, so I don't know why I was hearing this sound.

"And I looked down and I could see I was naked. I could see the tops of my knees and my pubic area. He disappeared around the front of me, and then I felt something. I felt something cold and wet. And then I remember seeing—ah, somebody showed me a knife, like a scalpel. And then a table draped in the same kind of fabric that he was wearing. I know this is stupid. I thought it was some kind of abuse thing, but I had no idea what it could have been. I felt as if it was a hidden memory. It's very clear. I can see it all now. I never lost the memory."

This account may seem bizarre and unrelated, however, clowns are a repetitive motif in many alien abductions. In another case I investigated, a woman had repeated UFO encounters throughout her life. One early encounter involved the clown motif. As she recalled, "There was this thing standing at my parents' French doors. Its face was like a whitish face. The way my mind made it look was into almost a clown-type face. It had black eyes. I wasn't afraid, but I was always confused to know if I was dreaming or not. I basically was convinced that I really saw this thing. And it wasn't like a type of thing where it was a person. I know that started when I was young. What I remember was there was a bush with orange flowers. What I did was I made it look like a clown because of the orange flowers near the head. So I always had a fear of clowns since that time, because it was like someone looking in my window, and why is this person dressed like a clown? But it wasn't really a clown. What I think back now, it was not a clown. But I was always afraid of clowns after that."

Another case involving clowns took place in England. UFO investigator Peter Hough writes in his book, *The Truth About Alien Encounters,* about two young girls, Stephanie and Janice, who had repeated UFO encounters, one of which involved the clown motif. Hough writes:

> One day they were playing in the gutted buildings when Stephanie and her friend Janice glanced through the broken living-room window of the house second from the end. Something in the room made them gasp. They called over the other children, but they were unable to see what had attracted the girls' attention. Stephanie and Janice could not understand why. Hanging in an alcove, as plain as day, they could see a baggy clown costume. They decided to investigate. . . . the room was black with mildew, yet in the midst of all

the decay the costume hung like a sparkling jewel ... a tomato-red satin costume with white spots and filly cuffs, ankles and collar. Suspended by a loop was a clown's hat with a white pom-pom sewn on the top. The girls stepped over the threshold into the room.

At this point, one of the girls reached out and touched the costume, only to discover that "as I did so, the costume shimmered." Apparently, it was some sort of a holographic image. The girls ran away in terror.

Another case from England involves an abductee by the name of Abigail. Under hypnosis, Abigail describes an entity in familiar terms, "It's white with very, very blue eyes. Its face is painted, some sort of clown with a big grin. It's horrible; I hate it."

Abduction researcher Budd Hopkins reports several cases of abductees with this same bizarre phobia—a fear of clowns. He writes in his book *Witnessed:*

> I have encountered at least five abductees with this same dread fear of clowns, in every case dating from childhood. Most cite clowns' scary, exaggerated eyes and the mask-like painted faces. It would seem that for some abductees, seeing the natural human physical body and/or face stylized or distorted triggers memories of the aliens' non-human appearance.

As can be seen, Laura's memory of the harlequin costume is by no means unique, and seems certainly related to her UFO experiences. Another strong relation is her memory of being cut by a "scalpel-like instru-ment." Her memory of "a table" is also reminiscent of abduction accounts.

Today Laura lives with her husband and son in sunny southern California. They continue to have occasional UFO sightings. Laura's husband sighted a glowing triangle while driving home from work. On another occasion, Laura sighted a bar-like object with a brilliant light at both ends being chased by heli-copters. Laura's son has declined to get involved, as the subject makes him decidedly uneasy.

They are simply one family out of thousands, or perhaps millions, who deal with the phenomena as best they can.

Night of the UFO

Seeing a UFO for the first time is a profound experience. It is at once humbling and awe-inspiring, frightening and exciting, mysterious and illuminating. It is an experience that can, and often does, have a dramatic effect on a person's life.

Jay Broman (who, in order to remain anonymous, requested I change his name) grew up in his rural home outside of Ann Arbor, Michigan. Not only had he never seen a UFO, he had never really given them much thought. Then one night in September 1978, when he was eighteen, he had a dramatic series of encounters that began with a close-up sighting of dozens of UFOs (along with hundreds of other witnesses). It ended with an event so mysterious, Jay is still trying to figure out today exactly what happened.

It all began when a local farmer on the edge of town reported he was regularly seeing strange objects over his farm. At first, no one believed him. But when some of the other townspeople went to check it out, they were surprised to see the farmer was right. As usually happens in a small town, the news spread fast. Soon everyone knew about the farmhouse, and eagerly awaited the time when the UFOs would return. Then one night, word spread that the UFOs were back.

Jay and his friend hopped into Jay's brand-new Ford pickup and drove quickly to the farm. He had no idea what to expect. It turned out to be an experience he would never forget.

Jay recalled how it began. "It started around 9:30 or so. There was this buzz about town that this farmer down the road was having regular visits over his field there. Several people had reported going out there and confirming this. So a fellow artist and I, we decided to drive to this farmhouse about a couple of miles down the road in rural Michigan, outside of Pinckney, Michigan. It's southwest of Ann Arbor about twenty miles . . . out in the middle of cow country there.

"So we drove up to this farmer's area, and all of a sudden, I noticed there were cars on both sides of the road. It was like people were going to see some kind of summer festival or something. There was no parking, so they parked on the road. And the parking was going back a quarter mile from the place! We got out of the car and started walking up, and there was a whole bunch of people walking that way, but nobody saying a word. Nobody was stopping to [ask] why they were there, but we were all there for the same reason.

"So I walked up there, and when we finally got up there, there was like three hundred people or something like that, standing around. And they had a little remote camera, and they had a newsstand there, and they were doing an interview with the local news guy. 'We're here at Joe's farm . . . blah, blah, blah . . .' Channel Seven of Detroit, I think was doing it, ABC, their big network. And sure as hell, about fifteen minutes after we got up there, coming from the north and coming directly south in line with this guy's field was what appeared to be a grid, forty different vehicles. I guess I'd call them 'vehicles,' and spinning in color. They kind of moved as one, in a matrix type of grid, filling out a square. And I remember them being red and yellow and kind of marbling their color. Their lights were bright, but they kind of marbled and changed. It was almost like a lava lamp."

Jay estimated that the objects were about three miles distant and at least a quarter of a mile across. He reported that the objects hovered in perfect silence. It was as though the objects (or the occupants inside the objects) knew that a crowd of people were observing them, and they were obliging a sort of display. Jay wasn't sure if there was one large object or a number of small ones moving in unison. At times the object or objects would appear to move slowly and then come quite close to the crowd. The lights appeared to be slightly larger and brighter than the stars and were vividly colored. He did notice that the objects moved very strangely. "It moved like it was one, almost like a circuit board. They all moved together, like they were all bound by something that kept them equidistant in their movements."

As the crowd watched, something very strange happened. Instead of getting excited about what they were seeing, everybody seemed to become enveloped into a strange state of denial or even casual acceptance, as if seeing what appeared to be alien spacecraft was a normal everyday occurrence. Jay remembered, "Everybody looked up there, and it was a kind of strange scene. Nobody was freaking out and going 'ooh' and 'ahh!' Even myself, it was kind of like there was this weird psychology or hypnotic effect to it, like, 'Oh, yeah, that's nice.' Then people got in their cars and left, like it was no big deal. You would think they would have freaked out on this; it's one of the biggest things I've ever come in contact with. We got tired and left. They were still there when we left. We didn't care anymore. . . . Everybody saw it and they took pictures of it, and no big deal. We just left. I mean, that sounds pretty strange, doesn't it?"

Actually, this strange effect has been a factor in many other UFO sightings. Investigators are unsure whether it is a phenomenon imposed upon the witnesses by the objects, or simply a psychological reaction to a very unusual event. Whatever the reason, it turns up again and again. Immediately following an encounter, the witnesses react as if there was no encounter at all, and often do not even discuss the incident.

Jay and his friend drove away like all the others, not really even thinking about what they had just seen. His friend lived of the M-36 freeway, about a mile down a dirt road. The terrain was hilly, wooded, and very remote. Jay dropped his friend off at his home, and then headed back toward the main highway. He assumed that the night's experiences were over. No sooner had he left his friend's house and started down the dirt road, he saw another object.

"Coming back there," he recalled. "I saw this—it looked like a helicopter or something, shining a light down into the trees. Now this was way out in the middle of nowhere. They don't just take helicopters out there, especially at night, and look around. It's just the woods. They're not going to find anything but a raccoon. . . . I just saw like little landing lights, but the main beam was going into the trees, and it

was moving around like it was looking for something or someone. And I'm thinking, 'Oh, cool!'

"It was a long shot, but we just saw these UFOs, and
I'm thinking, 'Hey, I just got a feeling.' I was going
over this field towards it. My truck is now heading
with the headlights towards this thing over the trees.
And I quickly flipped my high beams on and off several times, like, 'I'll get its attention!'

"So I got to the intersection where this dirt road
hits the main road. It's like a two-lane highway. You
can go fifty-five [miles per hour], but it's only two
lanes. It's out in the middle of nowhere. It's not developed. And the thing seemed to react to me. But it was
moving very slowly. And I got out of the truck at that
point, and I heard what sounded like a hovercraft
engine. It didn't sound like a helicopter. There was no
'chop-chop-chop' sound. You know, the noise of a helicopter, 'chk-chk-chk'? That wasn't there. It was just like
a 'brrrrr,' a low vibration. And the vibration would
raise in pitch a little bit and it would get higher. It
would rise up in altitude, like a balloon almost. It was
that graceful. But when it would get low again, it
would drop down again. It kind of reacted to me, but
then it just kept getting out to—I believe it would have
been the east. This main highway was going east and
west, and I was headed east. It just took off and went
back looking through the east."

Jay's decision to flick his high beams on and off was probably the point of no return. It was this action that likely turned the encounter from a mere sighting to one involving a closer interaction between the object and the witness. Judging from what occurred after this flicking of the high beams, this seems to be the case.

Jay estimates that the object was less than a mile away from him. He was sure it wasn't a helicopter, not only because a helicopter would never be out there in the wilderness, but because it moved strangely and sounded even stranger. He couldn't imagine what the craft was doing out there. He was quite surprised when it actually reacted to his presence. "It seemed to come closer, but then it just turned around and kept looking for rabbits and the trees or whatever. I don't know what the heck it was looking for. There were no houses. It was just state land, a wooded area. There were a lot of power lines out there, that's about it. So I just kept going east, thinking, 'That was pretty weird,' and I kind of forgot about it."

By now it was just past 11:00 P.M. Jay was surprised to have had two UFO experiences one right after the other. The chances of that seemed remote. But he had no doubt that what he had seen was very strange. Not only that, but it had reacted to his presence. He never felt any fear, but then the object never got very close to him. He was very excited, but also felt strangely calm.

Again he assumed that his experiences with UFOs were over. As he continued on his way down the lonely country road, he had no idea that he was about to have yet another dramatic sighting.

Jay recalled, "I started driving east and about four or five miles down the road I came across where my high school was located, on the left side of the road. And I see this thing kind of over the football field. So I pulled off and I got out of the truck again and looked, and this thing passed right over me. But it was way up there, like a mile or two up there. But it passed over me. It was really big, but it was so far up. . . . It just looked like a big black rectangle, like a domino floating. I didn't know what it was. I knew we had military bases out there, still I didn't know; maybe it wasn't human, you know? And it passed off and went to the northeast or wherever, so I lost it again."

By now, Jay was thoroughly amazed. What was going on? Why was he seeing so many strange objects in the sky? It seemed like an invasion from outer space. Three encounters in one night! He could hardly believe it.

He got back in his car and continued driving. He couldn't wait to get home and tell his mother what he had seen. In his hurry to get home, he decided to take a shortcut. The shortcut was way off the main road, but it shortened the trip considerably. It was a route he had traveled many times, only this time, something would happen that would make him think twice about traveling that route again. Jay was about to drive into the strangest and most terrifying ordeal of his entire life. His first three sightings were obviously connected to what would happen next.

"I took off down the road," Jay remembered. "And about another eight miles down the road, I came to a diagonal intersection going across state land. It was a shortcut to get where I lived. I could go way out a couple of miles and make a right turn and come back, or I could take this diagonal road through a secluded country area. It was just a dirt road going back into the country, the farmland.

"So I decided to go down there. I loved going down this road. There are no cops, no houses, so I just went speeding on through there, throwing up the dust. It was a fun 'kid thing' to do. So I made the right turn and cruised down into there and got in there two or three miles. And I looked into my rearview mirror as I'm driving . . . and I don't know how to really explain this kind of weird situation.

"I noticed the stars in the sky. It was a clear, cloudless night, a beautiful clear night. . . . And I noticed that the stars were kind of being blackened out by something. And the trees weren't that high.

"[It was] behind me. I'm driving fifty-five miles per hour down this unlit country road. The only thing I had on was my headlights. A dirt road covered with gravel way out in the woods. And I noticed that, systematically, the stars were disappearing. So I slowed down and noticed the stars completely disappeared. I thought that was kind of weird. I had just seen these UFOs. So I slowed down the truck. I looked in my rearview mirror and I thought I saw some kind of light, or something on whatever it was behind me. I thought, 'Man, what the hell?!'

"So I slowed the truck and stopped, and all the dust kind of crawled up behind me. When I stopped, it all caught up to me. But I put it in *park* and I got out. And the same thing that I had seen over the high school was now descended down to about fifty yards above my head!

"It was behind me, but it was approaching me. My first reaction was, 'Wow, this is great! Come here!' And then it got closer and I started to realize how darn big it was. I mean, this thing would have dwarfed our field. I think they could have put thirty or forty thousand human beings in this son of a gun. [It was] just a big, domino, square thing. And lights would come on intermittently, not high beam lights or anything like that, just like back porch lights or something. . . . The lighting had a powdery, fluorescent hue. It wasn't real clear lighting. There was red and orange and green and white and blue, whatever it wanted to be. And it changed all the time, almost like driven by an intelligence or a computer. The lights jumped around wherever they wanted to go. They didn't stay in one place. They either weren't fixed or there was a lot of them. . . . Because they could turn the lights on however they wanted.

"And this thing dropped down on me and then it wasn't funny anymore. I started to really get a weird fear . . . And then I noticed as it was coming in, my hair started to kind of react, not majorly, but it started to stand up as if I had rubbed a balloon against a polyester shirt or something. I had this static electricity that was pulling my hair a little bit, and I felt like I had goosebumps on me. The hair on my arms stood up even. I think that's what it was. The headlights of the truck kind of browned; they dimmed.

"I was stopped and I walked around the front of the truck and was in the headlight beams of the truck. I don't remember if the engine stopped or not. Maybe it did. I wasn't thinking about it at the time, if you know what I mean. It was like I had been shot up with some kind of painkiller or something, like I had morphine coming in me. And I don't think it was the vehicle. I think it was my own fear blanking me out, going, 'Oh, my God!' Because this thing could have landed right on top of me. That's what it looked like it was going to do, just crush me.

"At its closest point, it stopped directly overhead of me, and I'd say it was just about fifty yards up there. It just covered this whole parcel of land. It was like having some major building turned sideways and held over your head, ready to drop. If you had the UN building, it was about that size. And if you turned it on its side and floated it like a domino in they sky, it was about that kind of size.

"So I was out of my truck in front of it before this thing really came down over me. . . . but it was a very large ship. This thing was bigger than a battleship. It weighed probably thousands of tons, and it was just hovering. . . .

"And then, right about in the center of it, like if you were going to make a holy cross, right where the center of the cross came together, a light came on. It was like a greenish, grayish hue, almost chalky, almost smoky. And it shined on me. And I felt almost like something went through me. I don't mean like an object; I mean more like I was scanned with some kind of heavy-duty x-ray or something. . . . It was a thin light. It was almost like somebody shining a policeman's flashlight at you. It looked like a gaslight, you know those real bright lights that they make with some kind of gas mixture. I just felt like something literally went through me almost like a radar or sonar beam that went, hit the ground, and bounced back up from me. You know what I mean? It went down, it came back up and returned to them. They read me somehow. . . . The beam didn't extend or retract. It was like our lights. You turn them on, they're instantaneously there. But it was like some special gaslight. It had a weird haze to it, almost like chalky but fluorescent. It seemed like there was a beam in the middle, but there was also this aurora coming out around it.

"Then I tasted almost like a weird metal was in my mouth. I don't know if you've ever drank certain vitamin drinks or something, or if you've ever had an electrical charge. It tastes like copper in your mouth. It was that kind of thing. It tasted like copper in my mouth.

"But I was thinking ahead of time. I checked my watch and I didn't lose any time. And the thing just kind of sat there for a second, and I heard the engines start to go up again, '*rrrrrr.*' And it lifted up and slowly went off and went looking around in the trees again. . . . I heard it increase in pitch. It started to go '*rrrrrr,*' and when it was doing that, it was raising up. It just slightly turned itself, almost like a balloon would, and it floated off to the southwest. Then it started about its business again. It had a white light, like a spotlight, looking around in the trees, like it was trying to hunt for grubs or something. It was really weird. Then it moved so far out, you couldn't see it because of the trees."

Jay was absolutely stunned by what he saw. It was so big, and the lights were incredibly beautiful. Whatever the object was, it was obvious to him that it was not from earth. Even the craft's metal seemed different from ours. Jay recalled its details. "The thing was just pitch black. It was darker than black. It was this complete void. But you have to remember, there was no illumination in that area. All I know is, like I said, I didn't really get the outline or depth of it as much as I did the fact that the stars were disappearing. That's how I noticed it in the first place. And it kind of like— I really believed it wanted me to get out of the truck so it could scan me. And then it let me go."

Afterward, Jay raced home at top speed to share what had happened to him. "So I got in the truck after this thing went off . . . and I rushed home and I ran into the house. And I'm like, 'Mom! You're not going to believe what I saw!' She thought I was smoking some kind of weird drug. And I really got hurt and disappointed."

Jay was shocked that even his own mother didn't believe him. Yet, he couldn't really blame her. He could hardly believe it himself. He had seen four UFOs, and one of them actually shined down a beam of light as if scanning him. He felt awed and amazed, but also confused and more than a little scared. When his mother rejected his story outright, he realized just how profound and unusual this event really was. Four sightings in a row! Jay knew that this was beyond coincidence. How could this happen? What actually did happen? What exactly was the beam of light that struck him? Were aliens from outer space actually interested in him? And if so, why him? Questions raced through his mind.

All these questions were overshadowed by the events themselves. The images remained vivid in his mind. The hypnotized crowd of three hundred people staring at the colored lights. The bright light darting through the forest. The huge craft cruising over his high school. The stars being blacked out. The beam of light striking him and vibrating through his entire being. And his mom discounting all of it as some kind of drug-induced hallucination. Jay's mind was going nonstop. He knew he had to do something to calm down. He decided to go into the barn, play his guitar, and just think about what had happened to him. Little did he know he was about to have an experience that would baffle him beyond belief. To this day, he is not entirely sure what happened.

"I grabbed my guitar and went out into the barn. We had a big metal barn. I got in there, closed the door behind me, and I climbed to the top of the hayloft and was sitting there playing the guitar. About a half-hour later, I hear the same darn sound right over this barn. I mean, I'm so high up in the hay that I'm in the rafters. I could put my hand on the roof. We're talking about a twenty- or thirty-foot barn. But it was all made out of aluminum siding—it was a big metal barn. So anyway, I thought, 'That's the same damn sound I just heard!'"

Jay sat listening to the humming sound for what seemed about ten minutes. The sound then changed in pitch and moved around the outside of the barn, as if it was looking for him, or scouting the area. Jay wanted to get up and go look for it, but instead he found himself reacting in a very unusual way. Just like his initial experience early in the evening at the farm on the edge of town, he felt a strange calmness descend upon him.

"There's some kind of weird hypnotic state along with all this. Because you're like slow and you're not snapping to what's going on. You can't seem to really put your finger on it. You are like, 'Oh, I don't want to think about this. I want to think about something else.' You know what I mean? It's like you're in denial or something because it's too much to really grasp at the moment."

After some period of time, Jay broke out of his trance and jumped down to look outside. That's when he got the shock of his life. He remembered, "So I climbed down off the hayloft. I put my guitar down. I pulled open the barn door. And like I said, it was a perfectly clear starry night. And I opened the door, and I just got hit by this wall of fog. This incredible fog just covered the whole section of the area that I lived.

"At this point, it gets a little fuzzy. I remember pulling the door open and this incredible fog hitting me. The next thing I remember, I'm up in the hayloft playing my guitar, and I'm hearing the sound move away. And there's some gap. There's something wrong there. It seems to me that I would have continued to investigate this. But I don't remember climbing back up there. I don't remember climbing back up. And I wouldn't have said, 'The hell with it.' I would have kept looking."

At the time, Jay didn't think about what was happening. It wasn't until many years later that he realized just how strange it really was. Was Jay abducted by aliens? His experiences that night certainly show many of the classic signs of an alien abduction: a very close-up UFO sighting, interacting with the object with his headlights, being struck by a beam of light from the object, hearing the sound of something hovering outside the barn, and most importantly, experiencing a period of missing time. All of these point very strongly to the probability that Jay's encounter is considerably more extensive than he consciously remembers.

Still, Jay has only recently faced the fact that he may have been taken onboard. After revealing his experience, I gave Jay some articles on UFOs to look over. One of them contained a checklist to determine if you are an abductee. Jay took the test and, as he said, "I was about 60 percent in a yes answer. Kind of scary."

Jay has no idea what occurred to him during the period of missing time. He still has not read any UFO books and has only a peripheral knowledge of UFOs, other than his own experiences with them. After hearing that many people have recovered their memories of missing time via hypnotic regression, he strongly considered following this path. Currently, however, he has not yet done so.

For many people, a UFO experience is a pivotal event in their lives, causing great changes in not only the way they view the world around them, but in their choice of lifestyle, where they live, how they make a living and much more. This was certainly true for Jay. His experiences of that night caused a huge shift in his life. A mere one month after that fateful night, Jay made several major changes in life. He decided to leave home and join the military. He enlisted in the United States Air Force, and became trained as an aircraft mechanic. This began a series of remarkable coincidences.

The first unbelievable event was that he was stationed down at Gulf Breeze, Florida, well-known as one of the most active areas of UFO activity across the world. His next assignment brought him to none other than Nellis Air Force Base, north of Las Vegas, Nevada, now part of the infamous Area 51, where the United States government allegedly secretly tests and back-engineers extraterrestrial spacecraft attained from UFO crash/retrieval operations.

Jay reported that his work in the Air Force took him to other UFO hot-spots across the United States. However, the entire time he was in the service, he never once saw a single unidentified object. He did have the opportunity to observe many unusual military aircraft of all sorts. Never once did he see anything that even remotely resembled what he saw back in Michigan.

Later he moved to southern California to pursue his career as a musician and actor. It was then that he began seeing UFOs again. Since October 1994, he has had UFO encounters on a somewhat regular basis. He doesn't know what it means, and he doesn't understand why he is seeing so many UFOs.

The answer may lie with his initial experience back in Michigan. It was as if, that one night, a door was opened. Ever since then, UFOs have been a growing part of his life. He still has trouble accepting what happened to him that one summer night, though he admits that it wasn't a negative experience. "If it was unpleasant, it was because of what erupted within my own emotions. And I can tell you that I really doubted myself after that. I had problems that still continue to this day. It's internal stuff that I can hardly put into words, but things in your psyche. It comes down to the denial. I still ask myself if the phenomenon is real. I say to myself, 'Boy, I'd really like to see a UFO someday.'"

Jay evidently got his wish. He has had dozens of encounters since then, and he admits that he gets the same feelings of disbelief and awe on each occasion. He is baffled that he continues to see so many UFOs, and is frustrated that many of his sightings occur when he is alone.

However, some of his sightings have involved several witnesses, and on a few occasions, he was actually able to videotape the objects, a segment of which eventually appeared on the television program *Sightings*. He knows that he is not crazy and just "seeing things." Hallucinations don't show up on videotape. Jay knows that he is really seeing something actually there.

Usually the objects appear very high up in the sky. Still, the sightings occur with such regularity that it has caused Jay to draw some incredible conclusions. What he has trouble believing, but can't help wondering, is that the UFOs seem to know that he is watching them. It is as if they put on little displays for his benefit, just enough to acknowledge the fact that he sees them.

Jay is reluctant to admit that his relationship with UFOs goes any further than that of curious observer, but he is beginning to realize that it may lie much deeper than that. Recently, on at least two occasions, he has seen small balls of light whizzing around his bedroom. At first he thought he was seeing things, but then his girlfriend also saw one. Jay has recalled no entities, but he does admit that he feels a very strong connection to UFOs. He is eager to see more of them, and with a track record like his, it is very likely he will get his wish. In fact, he might get a little more than he bargained for.

Most abductees are abducted multiple times in their lives. Jay seems to fit this typical profile. Without a doubt the UFOs are very interested in him. The chances, therefore, are very high that he will have further, more extensive encounters.

Abducted by Aliens

Pat Brown is an attractive woman who lives in a large condominium complex in a dense suburb of Los Angeles, California. She works as a professional massage therapist. Her life has, however, recently taken an unexpected turn. Pat had always been very skeptical of such things as UFOs. She had never seen one herself, and never gave the subject much thought. She had a friend, however, who was interested in the subject. It was this friend that sparked Pat's interest in UFOs, and sent her on an incredible journey she never meant to take.

The friend, whom I shall call Denise, moved to Prescott, Arizona. Over and over again, she urged Pat to come visit her. Denise wanted to take Pat to Sedona for a very unusual reason; she wanted Pat to meet some people who claim to channel extraterrestrials. Denise called them "walk-ins."

In 1988, Pat finally agreed to go. It turned out to be a decision that would change her life forever. Although she didn't know it, Pat's appointment to see the walk-ins would cause her to start having her own experiences with extraterrestrials.

"My first experience was . . . Sedona." Pat recalled. "I had a friend that talked about these 'walk-ins.' They would give private sessions. And she talked about this for three years and I never had an interest. And then, all of a sudden, I had this desire to go to Sedona and see these walk-ins. I have a girlfriend who lives in Prescott, Arizona, so I went to visit her. One night, I was lying in bed, and I had my back to the wall, when I saw these two aliens off towards the back of my head. I saw them come through the wall. And they came up to me. I didn't try to move. I don't know if there was any sensation. I remember just laying there. And they came over and they went in the top of my head. And it felt very good, so I allowed it. I perceived that I allowed it. And they were slender. They were iridescent, like a whitish color. And that was that."

It was during this time that Pat visited the people who allegedly channel extraterrestrials. "I went to see these walk-ins. . . . when I went to see the walk-ins, I said, 'You have a ship?'

"And he answered, 'Yes.'

"I told him, 'I want to go on your ship.'

"He said, 'You do?'

"I said, 'Yes, I'm curious to see what it would be like on your ship.'"

Pat said this only half-seriously. She still wasn't sure any of this was real. But then, three days later, she had a very vivid dream that she was taken aboard a UFO. In the dream, she was lying on a table and was put to sleep with a soothing yellow light. She is not entirely convinced, however, that the experience was really just a dream. She said, "I don't perceive that it was a dream because of the sensation I experienced with the yellow light."

Pat then returned to her condominium in Los Angeles, and assumed her experiences with extraterrestrials had come to an end. On Christmas Eve, 1992, Pat woke up in the middle of the night and found herself in the last place she ever expected to be—aboard a spacecraft surrounded by "small gray" extraterrestrials.

She recalled, "It was 4:02 in the morning and I woke up . . . to go to the bathroom. And I came back, got in bed, and I felt something pushing down on me. And I remember experiencing this before and thinking, 'Oh, now I don't want to go to sleep. And I woke up and I was on a spaceship. And she [the alien] felt female. There was no talking. And she was saying, 'I'm not going to hurt you,' She had her hand on my head and on my breast and she was saying, 'I'm not going to hurt you. I'm not going to hurt you.' And I was fighting her. I was fighting her like crazy. I remember sticking my finger in her mouth—the little thing that was like a mouth—and I was trying to rip it out of her face. And it seemed like I was going crazy.

"And the ship, it was small. There was real dim lighting. There were panels, like shelves, and everything was clear. And I was on a table. I turned my head and there was another entity. And this one was like a male, standing there—he was standing like this and he said, 'Boy, she's different tonight.'

"And there was this little robot going around the table and he was making sounds that weren't like anything I've ever heard before. But the ship was very cool, and it was very thin. The air was just like silk, almost. And the next thing I know, it's 4:20, and I'm back in bed. And I knew that it had been cut short. I don't know how I knew that, but I knew that it had been cut short. And I called my girlfriend up and said, 'You will never guess where I have just been.'"

Pat was understandably shaken by her experience, and the next evening, instead of sleeping in her bedroom, she slept in the den. To Pat's horror, the aliens began coming every night. "I went through thirty days of hell because it was like, everyday they were coming down. And I could feel them shaking me. . . . I remember them talking to me, saying, 'We're not going to hurt you. We're not going to hurt you. We're just here to talk to you and to help you.' They come maybe a whole bunch of days in a row, and then you don't see them for awhile. And then they come back again a whole bunch of days in a row, and then they don't come."

During these thirty days, other bizarre events occurred. Twice Pat saw a giant greenish apparition in her home. "One time, I woke up and there was this big green thing in my den, and I said, 'What the heck is this?' And I saw that in my living room. On two different occasions, I saw that. It was just like this big green thing. I don't know what it was because it didn't have any definite form. It was just like a big green blob. I couldn't see through it. It was like it was solid, because it was kind of like, not bright chartreuse, kind of like a dirty chartreuse-green."

On another occasion, Pat returned home to find her house filled with a foul odor. "One time, I came into the house," she recalled. "And the house smelled so bad. It smelled like someone had left garbage. And I was trying to figure out what it was. It was an awful, awful smell. But I perceived that they had been there. I perceived that that was their odor."

Pat continued to have nightly bedroom visitations. Each time, she would wake up to find several short entities in her room. Instantly, they would shine a ray of light on her that would leave her totally unable to move. These nightly visitations drove her to the brink of exhaustion. She was at the end of her rope when she prayed for help. She remembered when her encounters made a sudden change.

"It got so bad, to where I would wake up and I could feel a ray coming up my leg. And I would scream, 'I told you, you can't come in here tonight! . . . so that went on for like thirty days. And I remember, one time, I sat down and I was crying. I was saying, 'I don't know who to go to. This is just far too big for me to handle.' And all of a sudden, I heard this sound in my head. It said, 'Well, here is a ball of golden light for you. This is for your healing. As long as you need it, it's going to be here for your use.' And I remember it was like four days, all I did was sleep, and I worked with that yellow light, and I ate popcorn. So at the end of this time, it was like this thing went through me, this energy. And it said, 'You are on the yellow ray of healing now. When you're ready for the purple ray, we'll be back.' And that was that."

Pat was utterly confused by what was happening to her. She knew how crazy it all sounded, and yet it *was* happening to her. Her only consolation was that her terrorizing encounters had pretty much stopped. After she had the experience with the golden light, Pat's night visitations changed decidedly for the better. Instead of being terrorized, she had extremely vivid dreams of being aboard a spacecraft, and having positive experiences there.

At first, Pat again wondered if these experiences were just dreams, but then something happened that again convinced her that they were much more than dreams. Instead of waking up in the morning with dream-like memories of being aboard a spacecraft, she was able to go voluntarily aboard a spacecraft while fully conscious.

As Pat related, "I was having dreams and I could remember being on these ships. And I could remember seeing different colors. Sometimes I would see purple. Sometimes I would see red. And so I was laying in bed, and I said, 'If I go to the ships at night, I'm going to go right now, because I feel like going *now!*' "And the next thing I knew, I was on the ship. This being came over to me—it was like I knew him. And he said, 'Do you want to go to your quarters?'

"And I said, 'Yes.' And they took me to this room. And this was going in and out. Some of it I can remember very vividly, and some of it I can't. The air was very thin, the texture. Even in my quarters, it was real small. There was nothing personal in there. The shelves were empty. . . . One of the things that was really strange was the texture of the air on the ships; it's like silk—it's cool, and it's thin and it's just really a pleasant sensation. And they took me to my quarters, and I remember sitting down there, and there was this white man with blond hair. He was sitting there like this, and I was looking at him.

"And they came back and got me, and they took me to this room. I remember there was a table and they asked me to lie on the table, and I did. I remember it was a bronze-colored table. . . . they were teaching me how to go in-between dimensions. I remember things were happening in my aura. They asked me if I wanted to go meet the Master. I said, 'Yes.' And they said, 'Okay.'

"I don't know all that they said to me, but I remember them telling me there was something I had to do with my aura. I remember I went to do it, and I slipped and I was back in my bed. I said, 'No, I'm not supposed to be here!'

"They said, 'Wait just a minute. We're working with you.' And they brought me back to the ship again. The next thing I knew, I was like a mass of energy. I looked out, and there was this white man with yellow hair sitting on this throne. It wasn't the same man that I had seen in my quarters earlier. I said, 'Why do you look like that?' And he said, 'Because this is the way you want me to look.' Then he started changing. He became, like, a pretty color.

"What was predominant to me about that, is I was a mass of energy—and I remember looking at myself and thinking that I still feel the same. I still feel like Pat. And he said, 'That is your soul.' He said, 'That is the part of you that goes through all the lifetimes.' And then he took—it was like he separated the energies in my body so I could feel male energy and my female energy. He allowed me to see how it was segmented in my body. I can remember hearing his voice in my head. I don't remember what else he said to me. . . . one of the other things that they allowed me to experience was different vibrations. There's some kind of band that goes around the earth. They allowed me to see the thickness and texture of that band. To be there on that side, there was, like, oneness and peace. And when you come through the band, the vibration of this place is very thick and it's not a good feeling. Fear is what is predominant. It's like all you can feel. When you come through that band, all you feel is the fear.

"So then we went back to the ship, and we were standing on the helm of the ship. It was like I knew these men. I felt like I was one of them. There was one who was a male. It was like, 'I know this man.' And we went flying through the galaxy. When we stood on the helm of the ship, there was four of them in front. There were two rows of them, and I remember they were standing in front of me. They were standing like this, and the whole front of the ship was just windows. And you could look out, and all you could see was stars. And I just remember standing there, looking and thinking, 'Well, I'm home now'. . . and then I was back in my bed and it was two-and-a-half hours later."

Pat awoke from the encounter feeling great, like she had broken through a barrier. Her encounters were now helpful and spiritual, instead of just physically terrifying. Not surprisingly, her experiences had awakened in her a whole new awareness of spirituality. She felt that the aliens were positive and there for the express purpose of helping her.

An example of this came soon after the previously described encounter, while Pat was at work. She was massaging a woman when she felt a strange blue light come through her hands. In her mind's eye, she saw two gray-like beings operating dials. The aliens telepathically told her that they wanted to help her heal the woman.

Pat's experiences quickly became intensely spiritual. However, they are not without supporting evidence and even additional eyewitnesses. Because of her experiences, Pat had begun to seek out information about UFOs. She picked up a few books in the library and was shocked to see how closely many of her experiences matched the experiences of other people.

Then she read one book that sent her on a quest to actually go and hunt down UFOs at the "Four Corners" of Colorado, New Mexico, Arizona, and Utah. She didn't know how successful her journey would be. "I read this one book," she said, "that said they had an alien space station at Four Corners. So my friend and I, we were going to go out and see the alien station. And we're driving and we're getting out to Indian land, and it's night. And we see lights. And I said, 'Denise?'

"She said, 'Yes?'

"I said, 'Do you see that?' And it followed us for about an hour and fifteen minutes. We kept looking at it. It was spinning and it just followed us along the road. And we didn't pass a lot of cars, but we did pass an occasional car. I said, 'Well, Denise, they don't seem to be reacting to this. Are we the only ones who are seeing this?'

"She said, 'I don't know.'

"But no one else stopped. No one did anything. People just drove normally. So after about an hour, maybe an hour and ten minutes, the car started getting very hot. I said, 'Denise, I'm getting afraid.'

"She said, 'So am I!'

"I said, 'What's happening?'

"She said, "I don't know, but I feel it!'

"And then, all of a sudden, the ship dropped back. It dropped back to where—I can't gauge things—it was really far away, but it still followed us up the road. And I said, 'Do you think it heard us?'"

Pat is certain that what she and Denise saw was no helicopter or airplane. It was definitely unusual. As Pat remembered, "You could see a structure at times, not all the time, but at different times you could see a structure. You could see the form. You could tell it wasn't really large. And the lights moved around, like, circular, but there was also this panel of lights. There were lights that went around like this, but like I said, there was also a panel that went around. . . . So every now and then, the lights were constant, but every now and then, you would see this spinning."

After the object left, Pat and Denise turned around and went home. Both were totally convinced that they had seen a UFO. Pat was surprised that their efforts were so easily successful. She has expressed some concerns that she may have an implant in her body, and the aliens were tracking her. How else, she speculated, could the UFO have found them so easily?

After Pat returned home, she was to have another encounter with extraterrestrials. This one, however, was one of the most frightening and bizarre experiences yet. "The grays," as Pat calls the extraterrestrials, seemed intent on playing some bizarre game of deception with her. "I had a dream one night. I was sitting . . . on the side of the bed and the grays came in. I have a girlfriend that I'm very close to. And she was in my bedroom. And she said, 'Pat, I'm going to introduce you to your higher self.' And a little gray came around the corner.

"I said, 'This is my higher self?'

"And she said, 'Yes.'

"I remember hugging it. But now I know that they don't want me to have access to my higher self or why would they try to misrepresent themselves to me like that?"

Of course Pat cannot be certain, but she absolutely does not believe that her higher self is, actually, a gray-type alien. Yet she feels certain that this "dream" was more than just a dream. She was not aware that many other abductees have had similar experiences, during which the aliens appear to masquerade, pretending to be someone, or something, they are not.

As Pat's encounters continued, she began to examine her earlier life for signs of encounters she may have not remembered, or just tried to pass off as some bizarre event. She quickly discovered she had probably been having encounters for much longer than she initially realized. First, she could no longer deny that her encounters felt familiar, as if they had been happening for years. Second, when she examined her past for clues that might indicate an alien encounter, one particular incident stood out vividly. It was when she went to see the doctor, and the doctor informed her she was pregnant. The only problem was that Pat knew for certain that she could not be pregnant. But that wasn't the end of the story.

"I have seen the grays in my bedroom," Pat related. "So I'm quite sure that something has happened to me. I took my daughter to the gynecologist and I was telling them how I was feeling. And they said, 'Well, we're going to run a pregnancy test.' And I'm thinking, 'A pregnancy test?' That was on a Thursday. On Friday, they told me I was pregnant. I said, 'I can't have this baby.' My kid was sixteen or seventeen. I said, 'I'm not having a baby.'

"So I got set up and I was going to have an abortion the next morning. I remember my daughter went out that night. At 11:00 o'clock, she came in. At 11:30, I woke up in a pool of blood. I called the doctor the next morning. He said, 'Well, did you see tissue?' There was no tissue. He said, 'Well, you're going to pass tissue. When you go to the bathroom, just check yourself to make sure. You are going to see tissue.'

"I never saw tissue. And a week later, I called them back. I never saw tissue. And he didn't believe me that I didn't see tissue. So he said, 'Well, we will do a D&C [dialation and curettage procedure].' And he took me through a D&C. But now, when I stop and think back over it, it's like, maybe they [the extraterrestrials] heard."

Pat now believes that the aliens may have come that night and taken her baby. She continued to read about UFOs, and it wasn't long before she discovered that many other people have reported similar experiences. She also discovered parallels with other abductees. She read that many abductees report having strange scars appear on their body as the result of a UFO encounter. Pat inspected her own body and found a very precise-shaped scar on her leg.

As time went on, Pat continued to have further encounters. She feels that she is getting closer to being in full conscious control during her experiences. "I know that they were in my bedroom. I have seen them running around in my bedroom. It's like, there have been a couple of times where I could feel that beam pressing down on me, and it's like, you can stay awake just enough to kind of resist it. But you can't. I remember one time, I was waking up and I saw them."

Pat has come to realize that on some level she has probably given permission to have these experiences. Yet she says that she still feels violated. This has caused her to discover why the abductions are happening to her. She first went to a psychic, who told her to stop searching outside herself and to look within.

Her next step was to go to a channeler, someone who claimed to speak for extraterrestrials. She was in the audience, listening to the channeler, when a question-and-answer session began. As Pat recalled, "People around me started asking different questions about spaceships and traveling. And so I said to myself, 'I'm going to ask a question about alien abduction.' So they gave me the microphone and I said, 'Is it true that we make an agreement before we come here that our bodies can be used in this way?'

"And she [the channeler] put her head down, and she came up and said, 'One moment please.' And she was changing; a different entity was coming out and I didn't know that . . . because she lifted up her head and said, 'We are here. We are Zeti-reticuli.' She was talking like that [in a monotone, robotic voice]. And when she said that, this whole thing went through me—fear. I got afraid. Then I got angry. I'm thinking, 'How dare you come here?!'

"I went through this whole thing. They said that, yes, we did make an agreement. I said, 'Well, if you become consciously aware of the abductions, can you make them stop?'

"They said, 'No, you cannot make them stop, but if you become consciously aware, you will be handled in a different way.'

"I said, 'Well, what does that mean, to be consciously aware?'

"They continued, 'You need to understand why you have created this.' They said, 'We perceive we are supporting you in your drama. Why did you create this?' It's like they were putting this back on me. And I was going through so much stuff, I couldn't even think. So other people started asking questions.

"One woman said, 'You get so much from us. You come here and you get specimens. You take things from our bodies. What do we get from you?'

"They said, 'You get a jump-start in your growth. That's what we give you.' And someone was asking about emotions. They said, 'Our emotions are different than yours, but we do have emotions because we accept it as important to us.'

"They wanted to know how we perceived them. They were asking this woman, and I really wanted to answer that question because this woman was talking about conceptual love. And I'm looking at her, and I'm thinking, 'They come here and stick metal rods up people's asses, and she's asking them about love?!' I wanted to get the microphone and I wanted to tell them what I thought about this.

"I was so angry, sitting there. I thought, 'Maybe this is not the place for me to work out my issues with them.' But I did get the microphone back, and I can't remember what I said, but they said, 'Why do we experience resistance from you? We are curious. We don't understand that.'

"I said, 'Why?! Because you come and take me on your ship against my will.' And I didn't want to say that in front of this group because I didn't want them looking at me like I was crazy. But it slipped out because I was angry at them.

"And they said, 'There is not one person in this room that would not trade places with you.' I remember they told me—speaking through her, they told me, 'You should consider yourself lucky.' Well, they didn't say you should consider yourself lucky, but that the growth and the experiences you are receiving from this far outweigh the other things that you are experiencing. And there's not one person in this room that would not willingly change places with you.

"And I remember thinking that I was just so angry. So about two weeks later, I called the woman up who did the channeling session. She said, 'Oh, you're the one who asked the question, because they have never been out that long. They have never spoken that clearly.' She said she's been channeling them for just a short time."

Pat had yet another encounter in August 1994. She remembered aliens coming into her bedroom, but most of the experience remains shrouded in the amnesia of missing time. After that experience, Pat began to seriously consider regressive hypnosis to see if she could remember her episodes of missing time. She is fearful, however, that most of the repressed memories will be traumatic. She doesn't particularly like being abducted. She still considers it a violation.

She said, "This is something that I perceive right now. I don't perceive it as an agreement. If you do make an agreement, it's different here. It's so different here. I don't think you can be held to something that's made—I mean, if you think about universal law, there has to be respect. You have to not violate my space. I don't know if it's society that dictates that, but it seems as though there has to be some sort of universal respect where you can't just go into someone's place and just rip them apart.

"So this thing about the agreement, I don't believe that now. Even if I go deep in the deepest part of me, the violation does not feel right. It's like, if they came to me and asked me, I would say yes. . . . I don't think that they're here to hurt us or trying to do anything wrong. I think that they are here to do something that they shouldn't be doing. But look at what we do to animals. We have these egos about us that we are 'human,' and this gives us certain rights. But we now have people trying to protect the rights of animals."

Although she has traveled far, Pat still finds her encounters frightening. "It's something that I come home to and I have to deal with. I still sleep with the lights on. I have nightlights all over my house. And the hall light is on every night. So there's still an element of fear. It's not what's coming through the front door, it's what's coming through the wall. I don't worry about if the door's locked. I'm worried about what is going to come through the wall. Because doors don't mean anything to them."

Pat feels that her experiences have benefited her in many ways. Not only is she wiser about the existence of UFOs and extraterrestrials, but she feels that her psychic awareness has been increased tremendously as a direct result of her experiences. She says that her contact with extraterrestrials has left her totally transformed. "Five years ago, if someone had told me about extraterrestrials—my girlfriend talked about them for three years. I didn't doubt her. I did listen to what she said, but I never had the desire or inclination to go and pursue it. I never bought any books or anything about it. Now the way I see life is completely, completely different. I'm not the same person. I'm a completely different person."

After over a year of living with her encounters, Pat finally elected to undergo regressive hypnosis. Today she works closely with UFO investigator and hypnotherapist Barbara Lamb, a Marriage, Family and Child Counselor. She has had several sessions and has remembered a great deal of her experiences. She reports that it is often a terrifying ordeal to remember what has happened to her, but that ultimately, it's much better to know the truth.

Pat Brown's case may sound exotic and unusual, but it actually fits very well into the typical abduction scenario. She had been taken aboard UFOs against her conscious will on several occasions. Onboard, she experienced the frightening examinations that seem to be the focus of many onboard UFO experiences. Her case has supporting evidence including eyewitnesses and medical effects. Her descriptions of the gray-type aliens and the inside of UFOs closely corroborate with the descriptions of other abductees. Even her reactions to the experiences are typical—including sleeping with the lights on and her burning desire to learn everything she can about the phenomenon.

However, unlike many abductees, Pat has moved beyond the typical abduction scenario and is learning how to get the most benefit out of her experiences. She is quickly overcoming her fears and has initiated her own voluntary visits aboard the UFOs. She was given intensely personal and spiritual information, and has had unquestionably positive experiences aboard the aliens' spacecraft. She knows that her encounters are very profound and meaningful. Even though she still feels violated, given the choice, Pat says she would choose to continue to have encounters. Given the way things are going, it looks as though that is likely.

"It Scared the Hell Out of Me"

The alien abduction phenomenon is extremely complex. The abduction experience affects the witness on multiple levels. It virtually triggers the entire range of human emotions: fear, awe, shame, pride, humility, excitement, joy, anger—all can be part of the UFO experience. But emotions are not all that is affected.

A profound UFO experience also shakes up the intellect as witnesses are forced to consider concepts that are literally alien to their worldview. They are suddenly plunged headfirst into the world of the unexplained, confronting their minds with enigmatic and paradoxical questions, such as: "What does this mean?" "How will it affect me?" "How can this happen?" "Could it happen again, and if so, when?"

But this is not all. Abductees' whole lives can be changed as a result of their experiences. Their social lives can be thrust into turmoil, as the abductee runs the very real risk of alienating friends and loved ones. It is not at all unusual that the abductee becomes the object of disbelief, ridicule, or outright rejection and denial. Then there is the whole spiritual aspect. Many abductees come away from the experience with strong beliefs about God, life after death, psychic experiences, environmentalism, and other issues.

Without a doubt, those involved with the UFO experience are dealing with life-changing issues. Furthermore, the abduction phenomenon may be much more common than formerly thought—many UFO investigators feel that as many as one in forty people may have had an experience onboard a UFO!

William and Rose Shelhart know all about the UFO phenomenon and what comes with it—not because of what they have read, but because of what they have experienced firsthand. Both have had nearly the entire range of UFO experiences, from terrifying and chilling ordeals to healing and spiritual experiences. They have had multiple sightings and onboard experiences. Their story is among the most fascinating I have ever investigated.

William worked in the navy for many years. After retiring, he worked for the United States Postal Service as a letter carrier, a job he enjoyed immensely. For William, his experiences with UFOs began one evening in 1994 as he drove along a lonely highway in the middle of the New Mexico desert. It was a Friday at 8:00 P.M. on April 22, when William departed from Copperas Cove, Texas, and headed for California.

For a change of scenery, he decided to take the backroads. He drove through Abilene and Lubbock. It was around 3:00 A.M. when he arrived in the small town of Clovis, New Mexico. He pulled off to get some gas and coffee, and to call his wife. Because it was such a long drive, he didn't stay long in Clovis but got quickly back on the road.

His next scheduled stop was Fort Sumner. After a few hours of uneventful driving, he approached the exit of his destination. It was then that something strange happened. As William recalled, "Upon approaching the exit, I slowed down preparing to turn and for some reason unknown to me, I overshot the exit and kept going. I was puzzled as to what had happened, but decided it was no big deal as I could catch the next exit at Vaughn, New Mexico. The road I was traveling was a mountain road, only two lanes and hilly. . . . I had been drinking coffee because I was driving through the night. I hadn't drank anything other than coffee.

"About a half-hour later, I came up this hill. And when I headed down, I could see off in the far distance, a huge bright white light. My first impression was another car with their bright [high beam] headlights on. My first thought was it had to be a huge truck coming because the lights were so bright. And then a few seconds later, this light started moving in different directions—up, down, sideways, forward. . . . they started dancing. They went up and down, back and forth. And I thought, 'My God, what is this?'

"At that point, I was at a loss as to what I was seeing. It apparently was trying to get my attention, which it did. The closer I got to it, I became leery. The closer I got to it, it changed course, moved to the right-hand side of the road and came towards me and stopped. I slowed to about twenty miles per hour as I was curious. I had no idea what I was looking at. My intention was to stop alongside of it and take a quick look and leave. I didn't want to jump out of the car. Just before I got there, the light shot straight up into the air out of my sight. It crossed the road, came straight towards me, and just before I got to it, it went straight up into the air.

"I then stopped where I had last seen it. I knew better than to get out of the vehicle. I leaned over my steering wheel and looked up through the windshield. At that point, I received the shock of my life. That's when I saw it. It was a saucer-shaped vehicle hovering at about fifty, seventy-five feet in the air, and not moving. The only light visible was an orange hue over the dome. The surface was a dark gray color and rough-looking. The round saucer under it was easy to see. The craft was not large, maybe thirty-six feet in diameter. I looked at it for approximately five to ten seconds when the fear of the unknown set in.

"I decided to leave the area as fast as I could, even though in my mind, I knew I could not outrun this vehicle. I was driving a '94 Oldsmobile with power galore. I shifted into drive and pushed as hard as I could on the accelerator. At that moment, a huge bright light appeared in the rearview mirror. At that point, I went into a total panic. Every muscle in my body froze. I could feel my foot on the accelerator trying to push it through the floorboard and my hands were glued to the steering wheel.

"I glanced at the speedometer. It showed over ninety miles per hour. And on a hilly back road, all that I wanted to do was get that light off my back. . . . Before I could leave there—I mean, this all happened in—we'll say ten seconds—before I could sit back down in the seat, that's when a bright light came in through my back window. And it came right on in there. And, of course, I was frightened. I didn't know what was going on. I wasn't looking for UFOs. I mean, I had never seen one in my life. It just scared the living hell out of me. But that was the experience I had, and it was strange.

"In approximately five or more seconds, the light left. And in my rearview mirror, I could see the light moving off in another direction. I breathed a sigh of relief and kept going as fast as I could to the next exit. It seemed like such a short time to cover fifty-plus miles. . . . See, that's the funny part of it. The road that I was traveling was about an hour and a half to get up to I-40 which would take me straight into Albuquerque. And I swear to the God Almighty, I made that in *such* a short time. It's true I was traveling fast, but I wasn't traveling *that* fast that I could have covered that in, say, thirty minutes."

At this point, William began to feel physically very strange. He felt disoriented, confused, and frightened. But what was really bizarre is that he had trouble figuring out exactly where he was. The road did not seem at all familiar. There were no other cars on the road. Nothing seemed at all the way it should be, and yet he had trouble pinpointing exactly what was wrong.

Then he saw something that, even today, sends chills of fear down his spine. Peering ahead of him through the windshield was a sight so unusual, so utterly unworldly, he had trouble trying to figure out what it was. Rolling straight towards him covering the entire road was something that looked like an enormous landslide. As he observed it for a few moments, he realized with a shock that it was a cloud. However, this was obviously no normal cloud. It appeared to come swooping down of the sky and start rolling toward him. Its shape was very well-defined and it moved as if it was being propelled. But the one thing that disturbed him even more was the fact that it was heading straight toward his car.

"I felt I was in the car," he remembered. "I felt I was driving. But when I hit those clouds, and they started rolling on me—I've never seen anything like that in my life, where the clouds—it was just like a big rolling thing. And even though I felt I was driving on the road, a sensation of being in the clouds overcame me, as I could see them rolling at me very fast. It was not a fog as the night had been clear all night. . . . and the next thing I know, I was up in I-40 and I was in a rest area. And it all happened so fast.

"After exiting on I-40, I proceeded to the first rest stop and parked between two semis. I did not want to be alone. It was two, three hours later when I woke up to a loud banging noise. When I looked up, it was a large tow truck attempting to tow one of the semis away. I got out of the car and asked the driver what was wrong. He stated that all his batteries were dead. "I got in my truck and both washers and wipers were dead—a blown fuse. This whole thing could be a coincidence or else it was zapped with an overdose of energy or something unbeknown to me. The rest of the trip was uneventful."

When asked what he thought of the possibility of missing time, William replied, "I don't know. See, that's what was strange. I don't recall looking at my watch. I don't recall anything. All I wanted to do was to get to that rest stop. That's all I wanted. When I got there and I saw those two semis parked, I went right in between them. Because at that point, I was scared and I didn't want to go through that again. I didn't know what was going on. I'll be honest with you—I did not know."

When William arrived home two days later, his wife greeted him with a strange story of her own. She said that a few hours after he had called her from Clovis, New Mexico, in the middle of the night, something very strange happened. William said, "Rose said the TV was acting up, changing channels, so she turned it off and it kept coming back on. She finally got it off and the next day I checked and found the batteries in both remotes dead."

Yet that wasn't the end of the story. In fact, it was two years later that William received another shock that made him realize just how strange his experience had been. "Two years [after] my original encounter, I got on that road. I got there just as the sun was coming up and I traveled that road. And what shocked me is there wasn't a tree, and there wasn't a hill. And that first night, that's all I saw was hills and trees. Now I don't know, but that blew my mind. Two years later and I travel the same road, and all of a sudden, it's flat, straight, and no trees. I can't even explain that. I mean, I was totally, totally shook up from that because I know what I saw that first night. I remember going up and down hills. I remember seeing trees. That is strange, isn't it, so help me God."

William's story has all the trademarks of an alien abduction account. The first clue was William's strange impulse that caused him to miss his exit. He thought it was strange enough to remark upon this fact, but had no idea what it could mean. Unknown to him, many abduction accounts begin with powerful impulses that are often too powerful to resist. The UFO literature is filled with accounts of abductees overcome with an impulsive desire to walk or drive to an unknown location.

When William first saw the lights, he had no idea that it was anything unusual. He simply assumed it was another automobile. It was only after it started moving strangely that he felt any fear. As he says, it seemed it was trying to be noticed. This is also a common detail; UFOs seem to put on a display for the witnesses. Then, of course, there is his description of being struck by a beam of light, followed by an apparent period of missing time complete with the mysterious rolling ball of fog, and a "screen memory" of hills and trees where there were none. Then there were all the electromagnetic effects, again a common detail often reported in conjunction with close-up UFO sightings.

At the time of his experience, William knew next to nothing about UFOs. It was literally a one-night course in the most intense aspect of the UFO phenomenon. Looking back on it, William still feels the fear rising in him. "That night when I ran into that one in New Mexico, well, they had me. There was nothing I could do."

Like most abductees, William was also filled with countless questions. Why him? Would it happen again? Little did he know, his experiences had only just begun. Some of the answers to his questions may lie with his wife, Rose. Since she was a very young girl, Rose has had UFO experiences. She was born in Lithuania, where she spent the early part of her childhood. Then, her family moved to Germany, and several years later, to the United States.

Her first UFO experience occurred in the mid-1930s in Rotenburg, Germany. She was only four years old, and was playing in the woods behind her home when she suffered a terrible accident and nearly died. Apparently, however, she was being observed, and something saved her life in a very unusual way. She recalled, "I fell in a fountain [river] of icy water in the middle of winter. I was playing alone with some childrens' dishes, and all I remember was I'm drowning, I don't know which way is up or down. Then somebody pulled me out and didn't say a word. And when I looked around to see who it was, they had disappeared."

Rose was shocked but relieved. She was certain that somebody had saved her life, but she had no idea who it had been. It wasn't until many years later, after she had had numerous other UFO experiences and was eventually regressed to recover missing time, that the answer came out. "I didn't associate that with one of those encounters until my regression with Doctor L. S. That's when that came out. He said, 'It was one of your [extraterrestrial] friends out there.'"

At the time of the above experience, however, Rose had no idea what had happened, and just filed the incident in the back of her mind. It was about forty years later when Rose had another UFO experience. The year was 1977. She and her three children lived in a dense suburb of Pasadena, California.

They had just finished dinner when their attention was drawn outside by a strange whirring noise. The entire family quickly ran outside along with more than dozen of their neighbors. More than twenty people observed what appeared to be a classic "flying saucer." Rose remembered, "We all ran outside because it was making a noise, a whirring sound, like a *'whhrrrr,'* but different from what I could relate it to. Some things you can't really explain, like how do you describe the taste of milk? It's unique. Our entire family and neighborhood saw it practically ready to land. We all saw it. It was round and it had all these different lights and windows. We could almost see in them. [The lights] were like every color: blue and red, orange and green, just really strange. Some were on the bottom. It was like no aircraft I had ever seen. And I was raised in the war-zone overseas. But it really, really looked enormous. I don't know if it was just going to hover, or try to land. I don't think there was enough room for it to land between the houses there. It was not a balloon. It had a light beaming down too, and the grass died. That's why we were all impressed. The whole neighborhood was out. It wasn't just us."

Rose, her family, and the neighbors watched this object for just a few minutes, as it beamed down a powerful white light. Nobody was able to identify it. They were shocked when the vehicle started getting lower and lower, as if it were landing. But suddenly the experience was cut short by an unwanted visitor. As Rose stated, "It was starting to come down until the helicopters came. The helicopters chased it away."

William was not a witness to the incident. But after he met and married Rose, they both had one of the most intense UFO experiences of their lives. It occurred about one year after William's experience in the New Mexican desert. Rose and William were driving all night between Sedona and Prescott, Arizona. Sedona is a well-known UFO hotspot. Still, the last thing William and Rose expected to see was a UFO.

It was around 1:00 A.M. when they not only saw an object in the sky, but had a long interaction with it, ending in a period of missing time. It began in the same way as William's early experience; they saw an unidentified bright light ahead of them. Only on this occasion, it was high in the sky, near the zenith. Both William and Rose kept their eyes on it. As they drove along, the light moved lower. At first, they followed the light, but then it wasn't long before the light began to follow them.

William recalled it clearly. "We were coming up the hill into Arizona, and we saw this bright light. It was a big, white light. It was a bright, white light, and like I said, there's no way it could have been a star. Because as we made the curves going up that hill, it seemed to follow us. It seemed like every time I turned around, it was there in front of me. And then we followed it into Prescott."

Rose's version of the beginning of their encounter matches closely with William's, however, as with most multiple-witness accounts slight variations exist. "We had driven two days and nights without sleep," she said. "And we were exhausted and looking for a motel. But something compelled us to follow that light. It was like we were hypnotized. We had to follow this light. And I remember we almost hit a cow. And we ended up in this little town called Jerome, which I didn't even know existed. I said, 'What are we doing? We must be nuts! We've got to follow this light.' It made us chase it. And it kept playing games with us. It was no star, way too big for a star. Stars twinkle and so forth. And wherever these winding roads went, it was there in front of us. Again, stars don't do that when you change your directions."

Neither felt any fear. But they both felt that the object was keeping pace with them, playing a cat and mouse game—"now you see me, now you don't." This went on for about twenty minutes when suddenly, the object made a bold move. It came swooping down out of the sky and came in for a landing, at least, it appeared to be coming in for a landing. Then it did the totally unexpected.

As William remembered, "As we were coming into Prescott, Arizona, that light came straight out of the sky and went into the ground. It just dropped. All of a sudden, *boom!,* it just dropped out of sight. And that was the last I saw of it. Now from that point on, I don't know. I mean, I don't know where it went or what happened, but I saw it come straight down."

Again, Rose corroborates her husband's account of the light coming straight down and seeming to disappear into the ground. "It did come down in the middle of a field. And this is where we don't have conscious recall of anything else, except we finally found a place to sleep that night. . . . We didn't find a motel until like 3:00 A.M., and we still can't figure out how that happened. We must have spent some time there."

After the light disappeared, Rose and William don't recall exactly what happened. They remembered stumbling into a hotel. They remembered wondering how they got there and how it got to be so late so quickly. But at the time, they weren't thinking about missing time or alien abductions. It wasn't until after they returned home that they realized that there was a period of time they could not account for.

As time went on, they thought more and more about the experience, and they began to speculate on the possibility that there was more to the encounter than they could consciously remember. Because of William's early missing-time UFO encounter, they were not entirely ignorant of the concept of alien abduction. They had heard that some people are able to recall the period of missing time through the technique of hypnotic regression.

They talked about it and finally decided that they would try hypnosis. William, in particular, was tired of the anxiety that came up each time he thought about his first encounter. He felt that it was time to find out what really happened. It took some time, but they finally found someone they trusted enough to put them under hypnosis. Their choice was a well-known

European UFO investigator. They got together and brought a couple of friends who were also interested to find out what had happened.

William went first. Unfortunately, William simply could not relax enough to be put into a deep trance. Despite repeated efforts, he was simply not a good hypnotic subject. The fact that their two friends were observing the entire procedure also created an obstacle. After several attempts, the hypnotist, Dr. L. S., realized that they were simply wasting their time, and recommended moving on to Rose in the hopes that she would be a better subject.

As luck would have it, Rose turned out to be an excellent hypnotic subject. She was easily hypnotized and put into a deep trance. The doctor then quickly and skillfully regressed her to remember her encounters. It was at that time that Rose suddenly jumped to age four when she very nearly drowned while living in Germany. Under hypnosis, she recalled being pulled out of the stream by what she believed were extraterrestrials.

However, the main purpose of the regression was to investigate the Sedona encounter. So the doctor moved on and asked her to go back to the evening in question. Rose quickly obliged and began to recall the incident in vivid detail. She remembered the drive before they saw the light. She remembered seeing the light and being followed. She remembered the light dropping down out of the sky and heading towards the ground. Then she remembered what happened next. Not surprisingly, Rose recalled a very extensive UFO encounter, though the term "abduction" does not accurately describe what happened to the Shelharts.

Rose described what happened that night. "During the regression, I was describing things that I had forgotten even—the details of the town and stuff. We weren't kidnapped or abducted. We voluntarily boarded and we were welcome. We sought them out and we climbed aboard, not being abducted as 'in force.' I guess we were curious. We followed it that far, naturally, but somehow that memory consciously was erased. But it was like suddenly we were just in it.

"And I was asked 'Where was William?' Well, that's what [the doctor] asked me. I said, 'He's in another room.' And they [the extraterrestrials] were just saying that we are helping you . . . they told me he was in another room getting different messages."

Rose was very surprised by the appearance of the extraterrestrials. She and William have since read several books about UFOs and aliens, and are quite familiar with the various reported types. At the time of the regression, they had no idea what to expect. But somehow, she thought aliens would look very different from humans. This turned out not to be the case. As she said, "They looked a lot more like people than some of those sketches do. *A lot* more. Their eyes were a little larger than any white person's big eyes would be, but they were just not enormous. They looked very much like they could pass for us if they wished. And they glowed with a blue aura which made me feel reassured, kind of on a mental level, that they were peaceful."

When asked how they were dressed, Rose replied, "Something like a military outfit, but not anything I have ever seen, and I've been in Europe and here, and so forth. But it would resemble that because they were all alike, but more loose fitting, but with belts. Uniforms, but it looked structured more, like, 'I mean business.'"

Rose was mesmerized by the appearance of the inside of the craft. It was very clean. But she expected that there would be all sorts of bizarre and alien-looking equipment aboard the craft. Again, this turned out not be the case. "Oh, there were all kinds of lights, but very few actual gizmos like we have on any aircraft here. [It was] like they didn't need them. It didn't look like they needed too many things. It's like they almost had mind control to get the thing going. But there were little lights, I guess monitors for whatever."

Rose was also told many different things by the aliens. When asked where they were from, the extraterrestrials gave a typically enigmatic and evasive answer. "They said they are from a place that you don't know about yet."

When asked about their purpose for coming here, the response was decidedly positive. Said Rose, "They said they are helping certain people here because they will help humanity. And something about like, the more we help, the more they help us. But they can't interfere and just take over and fix everything."

Rose doesn't remember much after that, other than suddenly realizing that they were no longer onboard, but were back in the car and approaching a hotel.

Rose and William can only speculate as to what happened to William. They were delighted by Rose's vivid and nearly complete recall of the event. They were also pleased that the event turned out to be completely positive. And lest anyone feels that Rose was fantasizing or being led by the hypnotist, it is important to note that even Rose was surprised by the results of the regression. She expected the aliens to look very different, and yet they looked very much like humans. She expected the ship to have lots of equipment onboard, and yet, just the opposite was true.

Of course, William was disappointed by his own lack of recall. However, judging from what his wife had remembered, he had no reason to fear the aliens. And as a result of her account, he was alleviated of much of his anxiety concerning what had happened. Dr. L. S. assured both of them that in his experience, which spanned over twenty years, the aliens were usually safe to interact with.

After the regression, they both felt a sense of closure. They had come full circle, from terrifying abduction to a positive interaction on board an alien spacecraft. They couldn't have wished for a better outcome. At any rate, they were happy. However, their experiences were to continue, moving, in fact, to a whole new level. William, it seems, had become of great interest to the extraterrestrials, for he began to have one experience after another.

His next encounter occurred again in New Mexico. William was driving on a highway located adjacent to Area 51 or "Dreamland" where many people believe the United States government is reverse-engineering technology gained from crashed flying saucers. I have talked to several people who have seen unusual activity outside of Area 51. When William revealed his own encounters in this area, I was not surprised.

He reported, "I've been down [to] Area 51, and I've seen things down there. The minute I pulled my car off the road, this was in the middle of the night, the thing [a bright light] just disappeared. I got back in my car, and I started driving. And it appeared again. So I know there's something going on there."

A year later, he had another sighting. "I went back a year later. Now this is something I can't even explain. I'm driving down the same road, and all of a sudden I see this red light in front of me. And I thought, 'Well, somebody's doing something.'

"So I sped up and this light kept moving as fast as I was moving. Now this is crazy. I know it sounds crazy.

So I sped up and I caught up to this light and it was moving right alongside the car with me. And we were going on this hilly road about sixty or seventy miles an hour.

"So all of a sudden, I found myself coming into this little town, I forget the name of this town right now, and there were these two lights in front of me. Well, these two lights went straight up in the air and went over the rooftops. And I thought, 'Oh, my God! This is crazy!'

"So when I got into town, I pulled into one of those convenience stores. There was a cop in there, and there was a clerk in there. And I asked them, 'What are these lights? What's going on here?'

"And they started laughing at me. They said, 'Oh, what did you think, you saw a UFO?'

"I said, 'Yeah.' So they told me it was something to do with the border patrol. They were using these lights. They were going to use them on the border with cameras attached and they were going to watch for [illegal border crossings] coming across. And that's the story they gave me. But I did see the lights. And as I left the convenience store, there were two of these lights, and they were in the median. And there was people working on them. So there must have been something going on, but that was on the same road, the exact road."

Judging by William's description of the lights, he was describing something entirely different from what the police officer and clerk were describing. It seems that they were talking about the lights in the median of the road. What William saw was completely different. Furthermore, the border patrol doesn't have flying cameras that pace cars at seventy miles per hour. In either case, it remains the most ambiguous and least dramatic of William's encounters. It wasn't long before he began having other experiences that were less ambiguous in nature.

After retiring from the Navy, William worked as a letter carrier. However, due to the stresses of the job, he developed chronic pain in his right leg. "I enjoyed my job or I never would have put up with the pain that I received from it. If you can imagine jumping in and out of a mail truck five, six days a week, using my right foot to land on for almost twenty years, and slipping, tripping, and twisting my ankle hundreds of times. So when I was offered early retirement in 1992, I jumped at the chance, as the pain was unbearable. Also my right wrist was in constant movement from reading and sorting mail, and [was] very painful."

It was a matter of months after his first encounter in April 1994 that William experienced another bizarre event. At the time, he was living in a remote and rural area of the Hawaiian Islands. Despite being so distant from the location of his first encounter, it seems the aliens knew exactly where he was.

He described the incident that tipped him off. "I woke one morning and felt an itch on my right foot and discovered three puncture wounds in a perfect triangle. They were in the process of scabbing over. I sleep on a waterbed, so nothing could have scratched it. My wife was the only witness. I felt something itching on my right ankle, and that's when I looked. Because there's no way possible in the night I could have done this, and that's when it happened."

William estimates that the marks were about a half-inch apart, forming a perfect equilateral triangle. It was very obvious to both him and his wife that it was not a random scratch. And yet, he had no memories of anything happening that night. It seemed totally inexplicable.

Then, a few weeks later, it happened again, only this time he was awakened by a very bright beam of light entering his bedroom. "A short time later, I woke in the middle of the night with a bright light coming in the back window. It lasted about thirty to sixty seconds. I froze and could not get out of bed to look outside. My backyard is a jungle of coconut trees and plants. As I live in the country, no car could get there at that time. When the light came in the back window, it was just as bright as could be. I couldn't believe it, and there's nothing in the back. There's no way a car could have got in there. I mean, that's what it looked like—somebody's headlight shining right into the window. And I remember waking up and seeing that. This was just kind of a shocking thing."

Instead of getting up and trying to investigate, William was unable to move. However, instead of feeling terrified and trying to stay awake to see what was happening, William unaccountably fell asleep. He never saw an object or any entities, however, it was very obvious that something was outside his window, and that it was very interested in him.

When morning came and he awoke, he immediately remembered the incident that had occurred in the middle of the night. He could only shake his head and wonder what had happened. But then he felt a strange itching sensation on his wrist. When he looked down, he was shocked at what he saw. "My right wrist was itching. The same thing happened—three puncture wounds in a perfect triangle. . . . I woke up and found those triangular pinpricks on my right hand. And this was the hand I used when I carried mail. This was in constant use. And they were very fresh, because you could still see, they had just about scabbed over."

"I showed them to my wife immediately. And I said, 'My God! Look at this thing! It's perfect. It's a perfect triangle.'

Immediately after these encounters, William began to notice a dramatic improvement in his health. He had already tried everything he could think of to improve the pain in his wrist and ankle. "I went and got myself a hot tub. I did everything I could to take some of that pain away. And it wasn't until after my incident that things started to get better. I just know that I progressed and started to feel better. Since then, I have been 90 percent cured. Only on occasion when the wet weather is extreme do I notice discomfort, but nothing like before. I am almost sixty-seven years old and I can hang off a twenty-foot ladder placing the weight on my right foot and paint with my right hand, day after day. I really don't care if people doubt my explanation. I know what I feel. And like I say, right now I'm very active in what I'm doing. Even though I'm retired, I'm constantly either working for my neighbors or for myself or whatever. And where we live here is right on the beach, and it's constant upkeep to keep these houses in great shape. So fortunately, at my age, I'm able to do this."

William feels very strongly that the improvement in his health is a direct result of his UFO encounters. As strange as this may sound, there are over a hundred solid cases on record in which people report healings either during or immediately following a UFO encounter (see also my book *UFO Healings: True Accounts of People Healed by Extraterrestrials*).

Another interesting result of their encounters is that both Rose and William have become very interested in alternative healing methods. Rose has become an accomplished herbalist-healer. William also has done considerable work in this area. As Rose said, "Both of us have become more and more interested in helping people in alternative healing ways. Even William, he has this energy in his hands that he didn't have before. He would just plow into your back trying to rub you down and almost hurt you. And now it's like I feel this heat coming out that's really good. And people say they feel it out of me. And I say, 'Oh, where did I get this from?' I have a lot of good result stories from the neighborhood. But I'm grateful, because I think it [the UFO connection] has a lot to do with it."

Since that time, William's encounters have pretty much stopped. At least, he is not aware of any encounters occurring to him. His wife, however, tells a different story. "They do come to him in the dream state. I don't care what he thinks. That guy gets flopped back in bed so often. And then he always tells me about this dream about aliens teaching him about different travel systems."

William also verifies this. "I know that my wife, she has told me a few times, she's thought that they took me some place. Because when they put me back in bed . . . and she said I came down, I crashed down. That's the way she explained it to me. Now, I didn't know. She said that I woke her up because it felt like somebody threw me in bed. That, I don't know. I just know what she told me and I have to believe her. Because she said she put in a hell of a night with me, and that's usually what happens."

Both William and Rose have also seen objects hovering over the ocean a few miles from their home. As William recalled, "They have been sighted here. There's an area, I'm going to say it's about eight to ten miles down the road. I know one night that they were sighted down there. They broadcast it on television that they had seen something out there. Now, I've seen something out over the ocean. It fact, one night about midnight I saw one. And we have a Marine base and I can see the Marine base from where we live. And they set out two helicopters and they circled this light. They just kept going around it. And then they went back to the base. So I know it was nothing [normal] up in the sky. It was something that they were looking at. I saw it myself. I was working late that time. I got home around midnight, and that's when I saw it.

"My wife has seen them many times. She would get up in the middle of the night, she would go to the front window and she has seen lights over the ocean two or three o'clock in the morning. They are in the area, but we don't know what their intentions are right now. But they surely haven't hurt us, that's for darn sure."

As can be seen, the Shelharts have had numerous close encounters with UFOs. William admits that his

1994 close encounter in New Mexico was among the most terrifying experiences of his entire life. Yet, like many people who have had very close encounters, he feels that extraterrestrials are benign, even friendly. He obviously has good reason for feeling this way considering the fact that he was healed as a result of his encounters.

Both Rose and William Shelhart have been profoundly changed because of their encounters. They now have an extensive library of UFO books and books about alternative healing. They are very active in their community when it comes to helping and healing. They are extremely spiritual and independent. Needless to say, they have a strong belief in the existence of UFOs. Together, they represent a good example of people who have evolved far in their relationship with extraterrestrials, and are true role models for others who are just beginning to deal with this most perplexing phenomenon.

Rescued by Extraterrestrials

Having investigated UFOs for more than fifteen years, I have run across many incredible stories. As a UFO researcher, I've talked to literally hundreds of witnesses. I have heard all kinds of stories, from simple sightings to onboard UFO experiences and face-to-face encounters with extraterrestrials. When I first met Sherry Jamison, there was nothing about her to reveal that she had had an amazing series of encounters with extraterrestrials. The following, however, is one of the strangest alien encounters I have ever heard.

Sherry is an attractive woman in her mid-forties with short brown hair and a wonderful smile. She first worked in real estate and became a very successful agent. Later, she returned to school, earned a degree, and became a psychologist and therapist. She has been married for many years and has a full-grown child. She is at once humble and dignified, with a quick wit and a positive, optimistic outlook on life. Looking at her, you would never guess that she has had many wonderful, bizarre, and even terrifying experiences with aliens from another world.

Sherry's first experience occurred when she was only eight. At the time, she lived with her parents in their modest home in the rural New Jersey countryside. One night in the early 1950s, Sherry awoke to find herself outside her home, standing in a field. She had no idea how she had gotten there nor that she was about to have an intensely scary experience. As she looked around, trying to orient herself, she glanced up and saw two strange-looking metallic craft, hovering about a hundred feet in the air.

One of the craft appeared to be very small and lower than the other craft, which was some distance farther up and much larger. Sherry had no sooner seen the objects when the smaller one swooped quickly down and started to chase her. Instinctively, she ran away in stark terror. Her terror became even worse when it sent down a powerful beam of light aimed right at her. Although she tried, she was unable to avoid it, and the beam struck her in mid-stride.

Sherry recalled the entire incident. "When I was about eight, I had an experience of being picked up in a craft. I was outside. It seemed to me to be a mistaken type of thing. I found myself outside. For the longest time, I wasn't sure whether I was sleepwalking or what. But there was this craft that was over on top of me, but there was another craft that came to pick me up. It put this beam on me.

"But the craft was not a very big craft. It was like maybe a two-man craft—a disk—but it was not a very big disk. And when I say not a big disk, it was not a mothership. And it wouldn't be like what I consider a scout ship. But what happened was, it put its light on me. And I remember running along the fence, trying to get away from it. And it had come down pretty close to be able to pull me up.

"It was about four or five feet in diameter. Not a big one—very, very small. But I remember running along the fence and this craft was chasing me. I was trying to duck down and this craft was chasing me. And like I said, it wasn't a big craft. And I couldn't get to the other side of the fence."

Sherry felt like a trapped animal. When she hit the fence, she knew there was no use running. Whatever it was that was trying to get her, there was nothing she could do to avoid it. Nevertheless, she tried running along the fence. Not surprisingly, the craft caught up to her and shined its beam on her. Sherry was totally astonished to find herself being lifted up off the ground by the beam of light.

She still had the presence of mind, however, to observe what was happening to her. She turned and looked at the object. Her strongest impression was that it seemed so tiny. She had seen airplanes and helicopters and even blimps, but this was much smaller than those, and very oddly shaped. She remembered, "It was a very small craft. It was not like I would visualize a craft today. It was about four feet going across. But I guess, to a seven-year-old, maybe it was bigger. But I remember thinking it was more like a toy, in my mind. . . . it appeared to be then, as a child, disk-shaped. Now, I'm looking at it from my perspective. This was very small. This was about three or four feet wide. And it followed me. It was silver. And on each side of it, it seemed to have something like—not quite a wing, it was round—but on each side it seemed to come to a point. On each side it seemed to come to a point almost like wings, but they weren't. It had one center light. It was something I have never seen before. And it seemed to have a ring also, something like a ring. And I don't know if the ring had any lights on it."

What Sherry remembered most vividly was her abject terror as she tried to run away from the craft.

She was running for several seconds across a wide, grass field as it swooped down and chased her from behind. Several times she tripped and fell, but her terror brought her quickly back to her feet. Although her first thought was that the object was like a toy model, she knew that it was out to get her. "It basically moved with me. I didn't hear any noise. It was actually like [it was] trying to make me stand still, because I kept running. It was chasing me. When I finally got cornered, I don't remember much. It kind of cornered me because there was a barbed-wire fence there.

"This one was a definite one that chased me. It was basically a chase. It just wanted me at that moment. I ran. It was overhead. It was high, but not real high. I would venture to say it was maybe like twenty-five feet up higher than me. It was not high in the sky. This was very close to me." Sherry was not ashamed to admit that the experience was frightening beyond words. When asked if it scared her, she replied, "Oh, absolutely! That's why I was running. Oh, yes! I was running and falling, and running and falling, and running and falling."

Sherry's last memory was being struck and levitated by a beam of light coming from the UFO. "It was like a flashlight. It was a very strong beam because I went right up into the craft. My sensation of fear left. I was so afraid when it was chasing me. . . . I didn't really remember what happened except that I was dressed differently when I woke up. I woke up with one of my party dresses on, and a pajama bottom on. And I had gone to sleep with a different setup on."

After she was struck by the beam of light, and lifted up into the UFO, Sherry evidently had a period of missing time. The fact that she awoke wearing a different outfit seems to confirm this fact. What happened onboard remains a mystery. Sherry has absolutely no memory of whatever occurred. She had no unusual physical sensations or unexplained scars. It was as if that portion of time had been completely erased from her consciousness. She did, however, remember what happened the next morning.

"I told my mother. She said, 'Oh, it was just a bad dream.' My party dress was all dirty. It was a pink little taffeta party dress, and it was all dirty. And she gave me heck for going out and playing in that."

Although Sherry's mother didn't believe her, Sherry knew what had happened was real. She remembered vividly running across the field and being struck by the beam of light. She also remembered the other larger craft hovering high in the sky. "I saw the bigger craft up there, but I was more concerned with this little craft that lifted me up into the light. I think there might have been a bigger one, but I can't relate to that."

Although Sherry's mother tried to convince her that the whole experience had been a dream, Sherry knew better. After all, she had physical proof; when

she awoke she was wearing a completely different outfit—dirty from her ordeal. Furthermore, the experience
was much too vivid and realistic to have been a dream.
Experiences similar to Sherry's have been reported by
many other people, and the details are incredibly similar. Of course, at Sherry's age at the time of the incident, she had never given much thought to UFOs, and
had no way of knowing that so many people had similar experiences.

However, because Sherry was so young, she had no
idea how to interpret the experience. She pretty much
took it in stride, filing it in the back of her mind, and
trying to forget about it. She had no idea what extraterrestrials were, much less UFOs. She didn't really understand what had happened to her, so she simply didn't
talk about it. After that incident, Sherry had no further
sightings or encounters. She lived the life of a normal
child, going to school, playing with her friends, doing
her daily chores.

However, as she grew up, Sherry had strange nighttime experiences, half-remembered dreams and recol-
lections of gray-type aliens standing around her bed.
She also began to awaken with unusual marks and
scars on her body. The experiences happened few and
far between, but each time it was more and more obvious to Sherry that something truly bizarre was going
on. Over a period of years, she began to wonder if she
was having regular contact with extraterrestrials.

Of course, this was no sudden revelation. She knew something strange was going on, but *extraterrestrial visitation?* That theory seemed so outlandish that, at first, she didn't even consider it. However, as the memories and experiences piled up, she began to wonder. Could it be alien encounters?

The more she heard about UFOs, on television and elsewhere, the more she realized that the answer seemed in that direction. However, her memories of the nighttime visitations remained very fragmented. If she was having a relationship with extraterrestrials, it was on *their* terms and not hers.

Although she had no complete memory of her experiences, Sherry had no desire to undergo hypnosis. From what she had heard, many people recall decidedly unpleasant experiences while aboard a UFO, and she simply wasn't sure she wanted to relive similar experiences. In fact, she believes that it may be better for her if she does not remember. What memories she does have have been tolerable, and she feels no need to change the situation. "I know what my experiences are, and they are experiences that are personal and can't help anybody solve anything. If they gave me some information that I could hand out or spread out to help people with their experiences, to make them more positive—but they don't. The only thing is, it's just that I've had good experiences, and I think it's what you make out of them. If I have been operated on, or [had] surgery—because I wake up with a lot of bruises and I come up with a lot of things—if I've had experiences that I'm being worked on and they choose for me not to remember it, that's great. I don't want to remember. Why would I want to remember something unpleasant? Why would I dig in my mind to remember something unpleasant that's going to make my life miserable? So be it. If I have missing time, I am okay with that."

Although Sherry feels she has been operated on by aliens, she believes that they are friendly. This attitude may seem surprising and contradictory, considering her childhood experience. Many years later, however, Sherry received startling proof that the aliens had her own best interests in mind.

It was the early 1960s, and Sherry was in a motorcycle accident. She was driving alone at night through the Watchung mountains of rural New Jersey when she lost control of her motorcycle and crashed. There were no ambulances to help her, no emergency paramedics. Because it was late at night and the road was isolated, there was no traffic at all, nor was there a house in sight. It appeared Sherry was totally alone.

Moments after the accident, Sherry did receive help from an unexpected source. Before the dust had even settled, two strange figures appeared on the scene. She didn't see how they arrived—they were just suddenly there. She looked up and instantly noticed that the two figures were not human. She instantly became terrified. The beings, however, only wanted to help her. As Sherry recalled, "When I was driving on a motorcycle once in the mountains, I had an experience—these same people appeared to me. They were like grays, but they were not grays. They were bigger than grays, more detailed, more white, not quite human. I would say, like, a body suit on a human figure, a white body suit, not a gray one, but maybe an off-white, or a beige-gray.

"I was riding a bike and I slid my bike. I had bent the kickstand when I did. I didn't hurt myself, but I had bent the kickstand and I couldn't move the kickstand to get the bike started. It was very dark. I didn't see a 'mothership' or anything. But again, I call them aliens only now. I always didn't know what to call them. They were just my friends. There were two of them. They looked at me and silently picked up the motorcycle, took the bar and straightened it out into a kickstand again. I nodded and kicked it. It was just, like, okay. And I kicked it; we didn't have electric starters at that time. I kicked the motorcycle over and off I went."

Sherry could hardly believe what was happening to her. Still, she knew it was real. She watched the two figures pick up the motorcycle and repair it for her. Without them, she would have been trapped overnight in the mountains. They came specifically for her. They never spoke or gave her messages of any kind. They apparently came only to fix the motorcycle so Sherry wouldn't be stranded in the mountains.

Sherry related, "There was no speaking. For all I know at that time, there might have been missing time. I might have been on board, but I don't remember. All . . . I remember is I slid my bike. And I wasn't hurt, like I said, but I was a little shaken up from the accident. And these two figures just came and one figure just straightened it out. Didn't say a word. Didn't exchange words. But I remember, he straightened it out with his hands. He just moved it. This was crumpled where it was under the bike where I had hit it."

Sherry has no idea how they arrived. She was sitting on the road next to her broken motorcycle and was trying to orient herself and check for injuries when suddenly they were just there. They stood right next to her, and because of this, she was able to observe them closely. Sherry is sure that they weren't human, and yet, they did have an almost human appearance. Their heads were not abnormally large as many other witnesses have reported, although they were hairless. Their eyes were also not large. In many ways, they looked much like us. "They were both right there," Sherry said. "They were about a foot and a half away. One looked at me. They both looked at the one doing it. They were both like the grays looked, without clothes. They didn't have any attire or anything on. They looked like grays except they were more human-proportioned. Except they did have the dark eyes, but not as almond-shaped as that. It was the only thing dark that appeared to be on them.

"And I wish now I could have not been so worried and disturbed, or that I could have paid more attention. But they weren't threatening. They just kind of nodded and went on their way. Like I said, I could have been abducted and not remember it. But I don't remember anything about it."

After the two beings finished repairing her motorcycle, they stood back and allowed Sherry to get back on. She quickly kick-started it. They nodded at each other and Sherry drove off. Sherry watched them as she drove away. "They were standing there when I kick-started my bike. And I looked in my rearview mirror, and I was so glad that they let me go. And then I looked and I turned my head back, and I couldn't see them. I don't know how they left. I don't know if they flicked out, if they walked into the woods. They looked almost luminous, but they weren't. So it was kind of strange. It was very strange."

Because of this experience, she now feels that the aliens are friendly. But it wasn't until several years later that Sherry started hearing more about other people who had seen UFOs and claimed to have had onboard UFO experiences. As the subject became more popular and accepted, she began to read about it, join various UFO groups, and attend UFO lectures and conventions.

She also continued to have vague nighttime experiences. It wasn't long before she began having other strange experiences, including additional UFO encounters. Since her experience in the mountains, Sherry has had at least two more sightings of extraterrestrial craft. One sighting occurred in 1991 in the Arizona desert. Sherry was attending a gathering of people interested in UFOs. She had retired to her cabin for the evening. Then, on impulse, she went outside to get some air. Suddenly, she saw a glowing red disk-shaped object rise up from behind a nearby ridge, about a half-mile away. The disk rose up, hovered for a few moments, and then quickly dropped back down behind the ridge. Sherry feels certain that the object knew that it was being observed. It was as if the UFO appeared to her just to say "hello."

A second sighting occurred about one year later in Burbank, California. Sherry was with a friend attending a local UFO lecture. They had just parked the car and were about to walk into the meeting when their attention was drawn to a large metallic-looking object covered with strange lights. The object was hovering low just over the trees across the street from the parking lot. Again, Sherry had the distinct impression that the object had appeared to her as if to say hello, that it knew she was observing them, and that they wanted her to see. Sherry also feels that the craft she has seen hold the same aliens that have been in contact with her throughout her life.

Sherry's experiences may seem unusual; however, all aliens are most definitely not the cold-blooded, emotionless creatures that they are sometimes portrayed to be. Many people have very positive experiences with extraterrestrials. Like the Shelharts, Sherry holds no ill feelings towards the extraterrestrials.

Sherry's experience shows that aliens can be very friendly indeed, and may just show up when you least expect it. She sees them as kind of guardian angels, or her "space friends." Although she has been chased by a UFO and has experienced missing time—although she has awakened to find aliens in her bedroom and has found unexplainable scars on her body—she still feels that the aliens are her friends. After all, they rescued her following a motorcycle accident. They have shown themselves to her on different occasions. They have caused only a minimal disturbance in her life. She has every reason to believe that they are benevolent.

Today Sherry continues to have encounters. She still has no desire to undergo hypnosis, but is interested in going out in the field and initiating full conscious contact. She has joined a group and has already begun doing live fieldwork in an attempt to contact UFOs.

The group has already had several strange sightings of unexplained lights while Sherry was present. With Sherry's track record, it appears her encounters will continue.

A Six-Hour Abduction

Recalling an abduction experience can be a tricky process. Many abductees merely see a UFO, and are left with missing time and virtually no memory of any onboard experience. Others are left with almost total recall of what happened to them. Then, of course, there is every variation in between. Some recall their encounters through their dreams. Still others elect to undergo hypnotic regression to uncover any hidden memories.

Then there is another method of recall. This involves a trigger mechanism that causes the abductee to spontaneously recall what happened during a UFO event hours, days, weeks, or even years earlier. The trigger mechanism can be anything that prompts the abductee to suddenly remember their onboard UFO experience. Some common trigger mechanisms include seeing eye-witness drawings of extraterrestrials, a close-up sighting of a UFO, or even just a visit to the doctor or dentist. There are countless examples, however, in each case, there are details similar to the initial event that cause the mind to suddenly jump back to the abduction experi-ence. It can be almost as traumatic as the initial experi-ence, causing the abductee to question his or her sanity. This type of recall is not unique to a UFO experience. Victims of any type of trauma, from childhood sexual abuse to war veterans, have had buried memories that surface years after the fact.

The following case involves a gentleman who expe-rienced a very intense missing-time UFO encounter at the age of twelve. His case is a perfect example of someone who spontaneously recalls what happened to him years afterward. His case, however, has many remarkable features. First, where most abductees experience missing time of twenty minutes to an hour or two, this man experienced six full hours of missing time. Second, there are other witnesses to the event. Lastly, there is physical evidence supporting the fact that something very unusual occurred to him.

The gentleman, whom I shall call Jack Stevens, lives today in Everett, Washington, with his wife and four children. He grew up on a farm in Napa, Idaho, and worked for years at a nearby factory. He gives the impression of being a very sensible guy, down-to-earth, confident and easygoing, definitely not the kind of person easily frightened—a normal guy.

And yet, he has had some very unusual experiences. For him, it all began one summer evening in 1972. Jack, his mother, and his younger brother, Dan, all decided to go to a drive-in movie only a few miles away from their home. The movie had hardly begun when a sudden thick fog swept quickly into the area. Within a matter of minutes, the movie screen became totally obscured. The theater personnel handed out free passes and sent everyone home.

Driving home was an ordeal in itself. Jack recalled it clearly. "I remember it being so foggy, and my mom remembers it too. You could just barely see each line on the road, that's how foggy it was. You were literally just driving from line to line. We were going maybe three or four miles per hour, that's how thick the fog was . . . we had to go real slow. My mom and my brother were in the front seat, I was in the back."

They were only a few hundred yards away from their home when things took a bizarre turn. Jack's mom stopped the car and said, "My God! Look out there in front of us. Have you ever seen an animal like this? Look, it's as big as a dog!"

"I looked and I couldn't see anything." Jack said. "My mom and my brother were looking at it. All of a sudden, in the headlights, my mom and my brother—I know this sounds really weird—she said it was a spotted skunk. I saw absolutely nothing. I was in the back seat, but I was looking right up their shoulders. And she and my brother are both seeing this thing walking down the road with spots. I saw absolutely nothing. There was absolutely nothing there.

"Right at that time that they were looking at it, the whole car lit up. I mean, it just lit up, literally. I can't even describe how bright it was in the fog. I remember I just lost it. I jumped down on the back seat. My mom said, 'Oh, look! It's a crop duster!'

"I said, 'Mom, that is not a crop duster.' And she and my brother are still looking up the front window at this supposed skunk that wasn't there. Like I said, I got on the back seat of the car. The next thing I know I just kind of felt weightless . . . everything in the car just felt like it was floating."

Just when Jack was getting a little bit scared, the light suddenly "winked out." The car suddenly started up and they started driving down the road. Jack's brother turned around and said, "See, I told you that was a crop duster." Jack looked at his brother and he appeared to be in a deep trance, with a vacant expression across his face. As Jack recalled, "It was just like my brother was knocked out with his eyes open." Jack's mother breathed a sigh of relief, and said, "Damn, that scared me to death!"

Jack tried to figure out what happened when they suddenly arrived home. He knew something strange had happened, but he couldn't figure out what it exactly was. He remembered the light hitting them, and then suddenly it was gone and the car engine was off. The only thing was he didn't remember his mother turning it off. He told her so, but she said that nothing had happened.

Jack knew something strange was going on. "We pulled into our driveway. I'm looking and it's morning and the birds are singing. I said, 'Hey, it's morning time.' And my brother gets out of the car and he's walking with his hands like you see in the movies, out in front of him, walks right up. Mom unlocks the door, goes in. I'm walking in-between them and I say, 'What's going on? Mom, it's six o'clock in the morning. Look at the clock.'

"And she looked at it and said, 'No, it's not, you're looking at the clock wrong. Go to bed.'

"I'm thinking, 'Wait a minute, what's going on here?' I said, 'Dan, look. Look right here at the clock in the kitchen.'

"He says, 'It's twelve o'clock.'

"I said, 'It doesn't say twelve o'clock. It's morning time.'

"He said, 'Whatever,' and held his arms out and walked into his room . . . well, the sun was coming up and I knew that something was up here. We were a farm family. We always got up early. Three or four that afternoon, the next day, I'm thinking, 'What's going on here? Why is everyone still asleep?' My brother gets up, no recollection of it whatsoever."

Since nobody seemed to think anything strange had happened, Jack mostly forgot about it. Like many UFO witnesses, they never actually discussed what had happened in any detail at all. As Jack said, "None of us discussed this after it happened. I didn't ever talk to my mom about it. My brother never talked. We just never talked about it."

Jack knew, however, that something very unusual had occurred. They had over six hours of missing time, six hours of which they could remember absolutely nothing. At the time, they didn't even think of UFOs. They simply never thought about what happened at all. Life went on as normal as before. At least at first.

Days after the sighting, another strange phenomenon began to plague the Stevens' farmhouse. Strange circles began to appear in the fields behind their home. "There was a crop circle made down there," Jack remembered. "At the time I didn't know what it was. I remember running around. It was about a three-acre wheat field. It had a spiral-type thing in it. I played in it afterwards. It was like a pinwheel on the Fourth of July, that type, with spirals coming out of it. But this was big, like maybe two acres, and it had smaller spiral things around it.

"I got blamed for it. I got blamed for knocking all the wheat down out there. Also in the cornfield — this happened for a lot of years. Right in one particular place, all the corn would get knocked down. And this was directly outside my bedroom window about one hundred yards out in the cornfield. . . . There were a lot of crop circle things going on in that area. I mean, there was a lot. I remember them always blaming it on me. My mom would say it was like dust devils or tornadoes, or a little tornado touched down or something. But I remember a lot of them. And like I said, that one stuck in my mind because I got blamed for it. And I had better things to do than to knock down about two acres of wheat in a circle. But I did get blamed for that one. And I also got blamed for the cornfield one."

The mysteriously appearing crop circles became another bizarre occurrence that Jack just couldn't understand. He knew that he wasn't making them. The complexity and neatness of the patterns ruled out the "tornado/dust devil" theory. He simply had no idea what caused them.

One thing he did notice was that they often appeared in the same general area underneath some high-voltage power lines. Another strange detail was how all the animals avoided the area as if it were some sort of toxic waste dump. Jack recalled, "I hunted bird down in that field a lot, and that area right where it was, was just like a dead area. You didn't even need to bother to hunt by those lines because there was not going to be any kind of animal whatsoever. And our bird dog would not even go over and cross underneath those lines right there. And there are other power lines on the road, but these are big ones."

Again, around the same time as the missing-time episode, a UFO sighting in the same area was nationally televised. None of them made any connection to their own experience, other than it was coincidental. "I know it was the same time that all the way through from Salt Lake to Boise, there had been a 'big ice-cream-cone-shaped' thing that was flying around at that time. I mean, it was within a few weeks of that . . . It was on the news in Idaho and Nevada. Anyway, it looked like an inverted ice-cream cone. A bunch of people saw it. It was all over in the news. This was like something that was on the Channel Two news in Boise, Idaho, where they had a picture of this thing."

Time went on. Jack continued to live life as normally as before. He went to school, did his chores, went out with girls, went hunting, and did other normal teenage activities. One of his favorite sports included snow skiing. Like many people who ski, it was a challenge for Jack to keep warm on the ski slopes. However, for reasons unknown to Jack at the time, this was a worse problem for him than for most people.

"When I went to ski," Jack said, "I would get like a cold spot in the middle of both my feet that just would not go away. I mean, it would be the next day before this would actually go away. I used to ski all the time, and when my feet would get cold in my boots, in the bottom of my feet, I mean, it would just feel like I had an ice-cold nail right in the middle of both my feet."

Jack had no idea why his feet would become numb for days following his skiing trips. Nobody else seemed to have this problem, so he simply attributed it to some peculiarity in his physiology. It would be nearly twenty years later before he got the answer to this question.

Still other inexplicable events continued in Jack's life. Like many people, the time came when Jack, then seventeen years old, had to have his wisdom teeth removed. This in itself was not strange. However, the dentist found an unusual object imbedded in Jack's mouth—something that had no right being there. "When I had my wisdom teeth removed," Jack recalled, "first he pulled out the four wisdom teeth. And then he said, 'Well, there's something else in here. I don't know what. I don't know quite what they are.'" The dentist said, "Wait a minute, there's still something else in there that's the same size as a tooth. I think it's another tooth." And he yanked two other things out of the top. He said that he didn't know what they were. He said they were really strange. He's never seen anything like them. . . . He pulled it out and he goes, 'Hmmm." I remember him telling the nurse to come over and he says, "Hmmm, look at this. What do you think this is?' And she says, 'I don't know. I guess it could be a tooth, but I don't think so.' And they threw it away."

At the time, Jack was just recovering from the effects of nitrous oxide (laughing gas). It was the first and last time he ever used it. But because he was still groggy from its effects, he didn't get a chance to examine the strange object or objects the dentist had extracted from his mouth. He clearly remembers that both the dentist and his assistant were bewildered by the objects. Jack had no idea how any foreign objects could have become embedded inside the roof of his mouth. If it wasn't a tooth, what could it be? He had no idea. It was just another strange thing that left him with a strange feeling, a clue that something was going on with him that he didn't completely understand.

Around that same time, yet another unexplained event occurred that left Jack a little shaken. It was during his senior year in high school. He was playing football when he suffered a severely broken leg. "When I broke my right leg," Jack said, "they did an x-ray on it and I had three clean breaks and three compound fractures in it. Well there's some kind of weird thing. They asked me if I had ever had a steel pin put in my foot, my ankle or my foot. They asked if I had ever had steel pins—if I had ever broke my leg before and had a pin put in there. And I said, 'No.'

"And they said, 'This is really weird. We got this on the x-ray. There must be some mess-up on the x-ray or something.' Because on my left leg there was some kind of a metallic type thing that showed up on the x-ray. So I'm wondering what the heck is going on here. Other than that, I don't remember what went on about that."

Again Jack found himself in the unenviable position of discovering yet another inexplicable thing occurring to him. First there was the missing-time UFO encounter, followed by the crop circles, and a UFO sighting on the local news. Then there was the bizarre numbness in his feet, and finally the strange objects inside the roof of his mouth, and inside his leg. Still, he had no reason to suspect that any of these were related or connected in any way. Again, it would be twenty years later when he would uncover the real reasons behind these strange occurrences.

From that point, Jack discovered nothing else unusual about his body. He grew up, got a job in a nearby sugar factory, met the woman of his dreams, got married, and started having children. The years passed and Jack lived a normal life. Still, in the back of his mind, all these events remained buried, waiting for the day when they might be satisfactorily explained.

It was in June 1997 that something happened. Spontaneously, Jack's mind went back to the initial UFO encounter on that foggy summer night in 1972. His memory was triggered by an event so commonplace that it amazes him to think how easily he had ignored everything that had happened so many years earlier.

It all began when he accidentally cracked a molar tooth. The intense pain opened a floodgate of memories that shocked him to the core of his being. The instant he cracked his tooth, Jack's mind shot back to that one night when he, his mother, and his brother all saw a UFO and experienced six hours of missing time. In a matter of minutes, he recalled most of what had happened during those six hours. Each time he bit down on the tooth, the pain brought in a whole new flood of memories. It was these memories that literally crumbled his whole foundation of beliefs about himself and the universe in which he lived. It was with utter astonishment that he realized for the first time that the object they had all seen was a UFO. In fact, he clearly remembered being sucked up inside of it and put through an ordeal that would leave him forever changed.

Again, it began with the 1972 sighting of what appeared to be a giant spotted skunk traipsing down the road in the middle of a foggy summer night. As soon as they saw the strange creature, Jack's mother and brother began exclaiming wildly. Jack, however, couldn't see anything. It was then that a bright white light struck the car and Jack remembers feeling a floating, weightless sensation. His next conscious memory at the time was the car starting up and then heading home.

But the cracked tooth brought to the surface what really happened. The light hit the car and then Jack felt himself being pulled out of the car and up into the air. As Jack clearly remembered, "The next thing I know, I just kind of felt weightless . . . I remember the car kind of floating, too, a little bit. The car was floating, like, side-to-side while my mom was still seeing this thing out the window. She stopped and the car was kind of floating, not really floating, but almost floating. And then when we stopped completely, it came straight up the road at us, and it was like two bright lights. Then they kind of came together, pointed right at us, and that's when I floated up out of the car. And I kind of floated out the side window of the car, which was rolled down. The next thing I remember is just kind of being upside down and thinking, 'Hey, this is pretty cool. I'm kind of, like, weightless.' And seeing my mom and my brother with just like a frozen expression, like nothing. I'm floating upside down. My mom, I could see her trying to move. And as I'm going up, I thought, 'Man, I'm going up! Wow! I'm going up into this thing! There's nothing I can do about it. I'm going.'"

As he rose up into the craft, Jack's greatest concern was for his family. "I remember saying, literally telling them when I was floating up there, 'Hey, I don't want you to take my mom or my brother or do anything.' And they said, 'Don't worry, we're not going to hurt you.' Well, not really said, but this was the impression that I got. 'We're not going to hurt them. Don't worry about them.' I remember looking down at my brother, and I'm kind of floating in mid-air. And he's just got this little stupid-looking grin on his face, just frozen. It was really strange."

Jack couldn't see what was lifting him into the air. Not only was it too bright to comfortably look at, but he was hanging upside down and was understandably disoriented. His next memory is of being taken inside the craft and floated onto a table. "The next thing I remember is kind of getting there, and one of them kind of knew me. I don't know if you would say 'knew me,' but knew about me. There was like maybe ten—I can't really call them people or anything, because they were like . . . entities. They were, like, individuals, but yet they weren't. And I don't know what they looked like. This is something that I've really been trying to remember and I cannot remember. I don't know if they were short, tall, big—anything. I just knew that they were there.

"As I moved around in the thing, I was realizing, 'Hey, this thing is big! This is really a big thing I'm on here.' And I remember getting on this one table. And I don't know how to describe it—it kind of like formed to your back. I kind of sunk down into it, but not really. And I remember getting kind of scared. I remember being on this table thing. Then, I remember two of them going back and forth, and it was, like, a 'good cop, bad cop' thing. One of them, for all he cared, just threw me off. That's kind of what the impression was, just like 'get him off here.' And the other one, he wasn't in charge . . . it's so hard to describe something that you have no idea what it was. In the meantime, the other one was saying kind of like, 'No, we are not going to do that' . . . this is what was going on. There was one of them that was like good, but he wasn't the boss. And the one that was the boss was kind of bad, but yet he still listened. I think they were going to really actually do something to me, but this other one kept saying that."

As Jack lay there on the table, the beings began to perform what appeared to be some sort of medical procedure upon him. "I remember them putting something in the bottom of both my feet. . . . I don't know what it was, some kind of thing—a tool-type thing, something in the bottom of both feet . . . I remember cold on my feet. I could remember something physically touching my foot, like a flesh-type thing, but not quite. It's almost like something was holding onto my foot, and then I remember being cold.

"And I remember them telling me to open my mouth, and that's it. Other than that, when it comes to the mouth part, I can't think . . . on that table thing, I do remember them being around me. But then they were kind of indifferent, like they just kind of watched, like a kid with a puzzle being done a hundred times, kind of like, 'yeah,' and a couple of them taking off, like they could care less about what was going on."

Although Jack was disoriented and shocked by what was happening to him, he still had the presence of mind to observe his surroundings. His first impression was the sheer size of the craft, which was easily as large as a small building. Everything about the inside of the craft, however, looked strange and unfamiliar. Even today, he finds it difficult to describe. "[It was] kind of beige. It was kind of all the same, like a beige, goldish, bronze color. Bronze, yeah, I guess it would be a bronze color, not shiny though. Like a dull bronze. I don't remember any sharp corners. It was smooth. Everything was kind of smooth . . . no sharp corners . . . [There were] no lights. I mean everything was light, but it was like—how would you describe it? Maybe like those hidden lights, like if you're in a room, you can still read, but—you know what I'm talking about, those hidden lights? There were no lights exactly . . . I remember when I was in the table-type room thing, it was just kind of like one side of it was open, but yet dimmer. I guess you really wouldn't call it glass. Almost like looking through a piece of plastic . . . it was kind of dim, but when I looked at outside lights, they weren't bright at all."

As far as the temperature of the craft, Jack said, "It wasn't hot, I know that. It wasn't hot or cold. It was just about right." Although Jack remembers looking at the beings, for some reason, he is utterly unable to visualize what they looked like. "Just for the whole life of me, I cannot remember what anything looked like there, any of whatever they were. They were there, but for the life of me, I cannot remember. I even remember thinking, I'm going to look at them now. And I remember turning my head up and looking at them. But I don't remember what was there. You know, I'm almost convinced that these things were ugly, that's why I don't want to remember them. I'm serious, that's what I'm thinking. I think these things were ugly, like scary-looking damn things. I remember not being intimidated by them because I remember looking at eye-level, or almost looking down on them. But then again, I was sitting on that table thing, so it's hard to say. Looking over at them from the table, I was trying to look for a way to get out of there. And there wasn't really like a door or anything. But there was almost like an escalator, but not an escalator. And it went up."

At one point, Jack asked again about his mom and brother back in the car. The answer they gave him was not very comforting. "The reason it was a bad experience for me was because I was scared for my mom and my brother. I wasn't really scared for myself at all. I was worried that they were going to do something to them. And I remember asking them, the good one, what . . . and he said, 'Don't worry about it, we don't want them.' It was like that. 'Don't want them. Don't need them. Don't care.' It was just like, 'We don't care about them. They can just stay there and they'll be fine and you'll be back.'"

As the experience progressed, Jack came to realize that the beings were almost devoid of emotion. Their thought processes were also very different from our own. "It was kind of like these things were like—I don't know—it's kind of like they were indifferent about everything. They had opinions, but I guess you'd kind of say they couldn't make their minds up, like what they were going to do next. I don't know how to explain this part of it. They were really indecisive, almost like they had to take a vote on everything before they did it. I guess that would be a good way to put it. Somebody would come up with an idea, then they would all have to kind of decide about it before they did it. That includes, like, even when I'm on my way up."

What impressed Jack the most about the beings was not so much their indecisiveness but their lack of feelings. "They're indifferent . . . almost machine-like, I'd guess you'd say. It was like no emotions. That's mostly what I would say, like no emotions. Like they could care less. Like just throw me out of the thing and it would have made no difference to him, that one. But the other one way saying, 'No, we can't do that.' But like I said, it was just like a jury on every single thing that the things did. Almost like whatever these things were had a card that said 'yes' on one side and 'no' on another side. Every little thing that was going to happen, they stuck their card up and the majority ruled."

After a while, Jack was floated up off the table and into another part of the craft. He was shocked to find that he never actually walked around, but was floated from room-to-room. "I don't really remember standing. I do kind of remember kneeling, floating, but I don't remember actually physically walking around in this thing. I was just, like, from one place to another."

What would happen next is unique in UFO literature. It would also be Jack's single most vivid and enjoyable part of his experience. Jack suddenly felt the craft move very quickly to another location. He could literally feel the motion of the craft. "I remember kind of shooting in this thing. I'm thinking, 'Boy, this feels really weird.' We kind of like went straight up above the fog. I could look out. The next thing, I was down in this thing. It was like a little clear diamond-thing on the bottom of it [the craft]. I'm in this thing and there are like bungee cords on me . . . I sat in this clear diamond-shape—actually suspended, it almost felt like bungee cords, but I could see everything around. I got, like, a 360-degree view. I could look everywhere. We drop back down and we're by my farm. We're literally down in the pasture above this ditch. And there are some big high voltage power lines, heavy-duty power lines through there. You can just feel the electricity coming off.

"Well as we dropped down to this thing, whatever the clear thing I was in, in the bottom, kind of got smaller. It was kind of like more of a confined space. It seemed wide open to me before, and yet I was enclosed, kind of like plastic or glass."

Jack was totally in awe. It was as if he were dangling outside the bottom of the craft, with a perfect view of everything for miles around. He saw his home below him and all the fields around. The room he was in seemed to be designed specifically for observation. In fact, the whole room would swivel to the direction that he looked. "In places it didn't move at all, like if I just wanted to look one way, it just stayed there. But if I turned, it would . . . move all over. But if I just stopped and looked one way, it would just stop and look one way. And I still remember the country. I was never up in a balloon or a plane or anything over our farm, but I remember exactly the way it looked from the air, exactly, looking down . . . I could see everything around the whole area of my farm. I could see for, like, two miles around.

"So anyway, as we went up there, the one . . . who was like the 'good cop guy' kind of starts telling me or showing me—it was like he was explaining to me what they were doing. And I don't know what it was. But we went up to the power lines and after we got back down and that little thing I was in seemed to kind of, like, shrink up inside, four rotating . . . things on each side of this thing—the diamond or triangle or whatever it was—there were four lights that started spinning around. And I could see them from where I was. But then I was back up inside. For some reason, I wasn't down in that thing anymore. I went inside into this room again, but yet we could see out and see what was going on. And I saw those beams suck all together, come into one big beam and hit the power pole, sucking the electricity out of it . . . and these were like, I mean, *lights!* They all focused into one and they started sucking electricity out of the power poles. I can't describe it but I could literally feel it going through my body.

"I remember being cold. That's when they went and sucked up that electricity. That is the most vivid part of the whole thing. And I remember we were up above it, a telephone-pole, maybe two telephone-pole lengths above it. And all those lights focusing into one super bright light—just *pshew!* Just literally seeing the electricity coming out of there, and feeling it. It was just like it drained everything, just took it all.

"Another thing, when I was up in that thing, we were above the fog, just kind of floating right above this fog. And when they went to go suck the electricity out of the power lines, that fog just got out of the way. It just opened wide up—just *shew!*—got out of the way, and I could see crystal clear.

"Another thing, I remember my teeth kind of hurting when it was sucking that stuff up. Just like when you're chewing on aluminum foil. I remember feeling like, 'Hurry up, get this thing over with.' I wanted to go back down into that thing where I was like bungeeing around . . . the one guy, the good cop guy, he was telling me all kinds of stuff, but it wasn't sinking in. I didn't understand what he was telling me. There were math formula things and something about a lot of triangles and circles. There was a lot of geometry thrown at me. And I'm just sitting there thinking, 'This is pretty cool, but I kind of want to go home.' Like, 'Get this done.' . . . The one that was the good one, was trying to tell me this stuff, and the one that was the bad one was not really allowing him to. There was a bunch of whatever they were in the thing, but there was only two that were actually—I guess you could say communicating or whatever."

After this episode, Jack remembers the craft moving very quickly to yet another location. "I remember just shooting off. And the next thing I know is we're, like, somewhere where I don't even know where we are. . .

we kind of shot around—like went for a little drive I guess you'd say—shot around. I can still remember the exact direction we took out there. The next thing, we were somewhere where I had no idea."

At this point, Jack's memory remains extremely hazy. Something else may have occurred, but he has no idea what it was, or how long they stayed there. All he really remembers is that the terrain looked totally unfamiliar. After an undetermined amount of time, they left.

Jack was somewhat relieved to see that they were back above his car. "And then we were back above the car, no fog. And I remember floating back into the car, just floating back over the car, right back where it was, floating upside down. I remember kind of playing around too, flipping, doing flips and kind of thinking it was cool going upside down. I remember getting to the car and kind of looking back up at the thing, and as I'm looking up at it, it's getting smaller and smaller. And I remember saying, 'You didn't do anything to my mom or brother, right?' 'Right, don't worry.' I don't remember floating back in the window, but I remember floating back to the car, seeing my brother, worrying about him breathing . . . I remember floating down, upside down, back into the car into the back seat.

"Then my brother just turned around and said, 'See, I told you that was a crop duster.' . . . Then the car started and we drove about a hundred yards and we pulled into the driveway."

Jack's memory of these events poured into his mind over a period of hours, however, each day that went by, he began to remember more details. Some parts of the experience are more vivid than others, but he is absolutely convinced that it was all a real experience. After recalling it, a lot of other strange incidents in his life began to make more sense. The crop circle patterns, the strange object that was x-rayed in his ankle, the object that was imbedded in the roof of his mouth, the memories of missing time, the UFO sighting that was on the news—all of these finally had an explanation, though not really the one he wanted. When he found out that his experiences closely matched other people's, his reply was, "Dang it, I wish you wouldn't have told me. I wanted you to tell me, 'Well, I've done extensive research and you're all nuts.' . . . I do feel better that somebody else has seen something similar, but I don't feel better that you came to the conclusion that we're not all nuts."

The flood of bizarre memories caused him considerable stress. Jack felt the compulsion to tell someone. "I was thinking, man, why am I remembering all this stuff? It's scaring the crap out of me." He explained briefly to his wife, who kindly believed and understood him. Then he decided to ask his mother what she remembered. Her response sent shock waves through his belief system. "My mom came up and visited a while back," he said. "I said, 'Mom, do you remember going to the movie theater and leaving about midnight, and all of a sudden, it was six o'clock in the morning?'

"And she said, 'You know, I've been thinking about that for twenty years. I don't know why I kept you guys out all night, and I remember leaving the theater.' She's been wondering that for twenty years why she kept us out all night long—and why it took us all night to drive four miles from the drive-in movie theater to home. . . . She just said it was, like, six hours that she should have known about, but she didn't know about."

Of course, Jack also asked her about the strange animal she claimed to have seen. "Do you remember some kind of an animal running down the road when we got sent home from the fog?"

She replied, "Yes, my God! I've been thinking about that."

"Mom," Jack replied, "There was nothing, because I was looking."

Her response was that it was the biggest skunk she ever saw in her life. She said, "You know, that is pretty strange now that I think about it, a three-foot tall spotted skunk running down the road in the fog."

"Maybe it was a Dalmatian?" Jack offered.

His mom said, "No, I remember seeing the tail."

Jack answered, "Well, Mom, I remember sticking my head right next to yours, looking through the window and seeing nothing."

She said, "I kind of remember that too, but I sure saw it."

Jack's brother's memory of the event was even more sketchy. "The only recollection my brother has about the whole thing," Jack said, "is the skunk. Nothing about the crop duster, because when that thing came down the road, my brother was already, like, gone. He was already pulling the blank face thing."

After the conversation with his mom, Jack was nearly devastated. It was not the response he was looking for. "Well, the thing is, with my mom saying that, you should have seen me. I darn near passed out. I'm a pretty tough guy. I was hoping she'd say, 'I just remember the crop duster flying over us, and you're a big chicken.' And when she told me that she wondered for twenty-five years why she kept us out until six in the morning, I mean, my knees almost buckled under me."

Now that Jack has received independent confirmation that something unusual occurred, he is no longer able to live in denial. There is simply too much physical evidence. Not only does his mother and brother remember the experience, but there is also the fact that some strange object was imbedded in his mouth, and he clearly remembers the beings asking him to open his mouth as they worked on him. And then there's the strange coldness on his feet, and he clearly remembers the beings working extensively on his feet.

The other thing that leaves little room for doubt is the crop circle formations that appeared in direct conjunction with the missing-time episode. Recently, however, Jack had another clear recall of actually seeing one of the crop circles from an elevated position. Then came a strange memory of why. He recalls the following event happening about two weeks after the missing-time episode. "I remember going to bed, and I'm thinking, 'I'm kind of going to bed early, but I'm kind of tired. I'm going to go to bed anyway.' And I remember my whole room flooding with light, just flooded. And I remember thinking, 'Oh, boy.' It wasn't like I was scared or anything, but like, 'Oh, God, here we go again,' kind of like I was annoyed about it. Kind of like I didn't—I wanted to go to sleep and I didn't want this. And I remember floating out the window into this superbright light right over the cornfield there, and that's it. I don't remember coming back in on that or nothing. God, I don't know. I'm feeling kind of silly about it now, but it's just such a distinct—I mean, I'm sure it happened. I'm sure I didn't make this up . . . when it did come back the second time, I think there might have been a whole bunch more [beings] in there, because it was just like, oh boy, here we go again . . . and you know, another thing, when the things did come back, I still remember having the feeling of just— I was kind of excited. I thought it was really cool. All I remember is my whole room being flooded with light and floating out the window. But I wasn't scared when they came back the second time . . . But then I have no other recollection after that other than just kind of getting pulled out of my bedroom window. This was just like a few weeks after the first time."

Jack also remembers looking at the spiraled crop circle with pinwheel shapes around it from an aerial point of view. The only explanation he can come up with is that he saw it from inside the UFO. "Here's another thing that's got me kind of weirded-out is, I remember looking at that thing from the air, but this was like after this [the first missing-time incident] happened to me that these came up . . . but I remember looking at it from up above."

Understandably, Jack has become increasingly interested in the subject of UFOs. He now realizes that he is one of those UFO abductees he has heard about, and is slowly coming to terms with it. He also continues to remember more and more details about his experiences. Like most abductees, he has had more than a few UFO sightings. These were simply sightings of unexplained objects, and at the time, he had no reason to believe he was personally involved and so just filed them away as curiosities—something you just can't explain. But now that UFOs have entered his life and hit home, he looks upon these sightings in a new light.

One of these sightings occurred in 1991, in the presence of his entire family and several other adult witnesses. They all saw what appeared to be several glowing orbs in a fixed pattern, moving back and forth in the sky. When Jack called the authorities to figure out what he and his family saw, he was politely brushed off; that is, until one of these authorities called him back, wanting to know more. "We were going to the zoo," Jack recalled. "It was just about noon. And I had [on] some . . . sunglasses. And I look up . . . and there were about seven or eight of these things that were in the constant shape of the constellation Orion, like Orion's belt. Three large things oscillating, moving. If you put the sunglasses on, you could see it clear as day. We were in front of an insurance office, and they came out and they saw me and my wife and all the kids just sitting there looking up in the air at this thing. Well they came out and they could see it too. The guy says he's as blind as a bat, but he can see those things up there moving. All of a sudden, the things all get in a big line and shoot off over the water. In about three seconds, they're gone, *'poof.'* So we're thinking, 'Whoa, this is pretty weird.'

"In the meantime, there's another little hotel by there. The manager saw us looking up there and she came out. The things came back and started doing the same thing, went back in the same pattern and started this oscillation weird thing. The bus stops, and right about the time the bus stops, the bus driver gets off because there's like six of us, seven, eight of us, standing out there looking up at the sky in the middle of the day. I mean, this was a crystal-clear blue day, not a cloud in the sky.

"Then here comes two jets from Woodby Island—*shew!* They [the glowing objects] get in a line again—boom—they're gone. The jets kick on their afterburners and head out over the water. No chance that they were even coming close to these things, anywhere close.

"The bus driver gets off and she says, 'I'm a religious person, and I don't really like looking at these things, but I sure think I'm going to be five minutes late. I'm going to look at this.' Well, anyway, we get back from the zoo that night, and I'm just thinking, 'What the heck? What's going on with this?'

"I called up Woodby Island, the Air Force base out there, on a Sunday evening. And I said, 'I'm just wondering if you guys are doing some tests or something.'

"'No, we didn't have any jets in the air,' they said.

"Well these things were obviously Air Force jets so there was no way around it. They were. So the next morning, my phone rings and it's Woodby Island, and they wanted to know what I saw. That was before they had Caller ID. I was just mystified how they got my number because I didn't even tell them who I was or anything. And they wanted to know what I saw.

"So then they tell me, the guy says, 'Well, I'm not really supposed to say this, but we had an airline pilot see something similar.' He says, 'I really don't know what it was and we didn't have any jets up there. So have a good day, Mr. Stevens.'

"All the kids still remember that one really good. Because they [the UFOs] just got in a perfect line, and just—*shew*—in two seconds, they were gone. You could follow them. They were kind of shiny when they were up there, but when they shot off, they were like a dark line."

Jack was more concerned about the fact that the Air Force obtained his number than the UFO sighting. The only conclusion he could draw was that they were definitely interested in UFOs and were using all their technology to study the phenomenon. This evidently included monitoring the origin of any calls that were made to the Air Force base.

In 1996, Jack and his son had yet another UFO sighting. "Me and my son were sleeping on our deck, and this cylinder-shaped thing goes spiraling overhead. I thought it was like a satellite re-entering the atmosphere or something. I called up the University of Washington Astronomy Department the next day, to try and figure out what it was. Well, first I called Boeing Field. I thought maybe it had something to do with them. Well, they told me that the Chinese had launched a missile that had burned up in the atmosphere, but that would have happened like twelve hours before what I saw. This thing covered the sky, and I'm talking big. My son saw it. It was like a cylinder-shaped thing, coming end over end. It went from horizon to horizon. I literally stood on the railing of our deck to watch it go over the top of our house. And I called them anyway, the guys at the astronomy place said three other people had called in saying that they saw something similar to what I saw. They didn't describe it as a cylinder. They described it as an orb."

Today Jack deals with his experiences as best he can. He is a bit in awe of the whole ordeal, and has no idea why it happened to him nor what it means. He doesn't feel it was a negative experience, and yet, neither was it something entirely positive. Still, he has not remembered any further details, particularly regarding the appearance of the beings. It is this gap in his memory that bothers him the most. On one hand, he is eager to know what they looked like. On the other hand, he is terrified by what he might remember.

An Alien Named Kevin

When people think of extraterrestrials, viewpoints often tend to fall into two major categories. Either people believe extraterrestrials are evil, bug-eyed monsters bent on abducting humans against their will and using them for their own nefarious purposes, or they believe that extraterrestrials are benevolent, altruistic, beautiful space-brothers whose only concerns are to elevate the spiritual awareness of all humanity and save us from ourselves. Of course, logic would dictate a bell curve, with aliens of all types, both good and evil and all combinations in-between. If one examines the accounts with an unbiased eye, this theory is strongly supported.

There is little doubt that alien abductions are occurring. Nor is there any doubt that some experiences are downright terrifying and malevolent, and yet some are even friendly. However, when people attempt to separate UFO encounters into one of these two categories, they often run into problems. This is not because the encounters don't fit into one of the categories. In fact, they have the opposite problem: many UFO encounters can fit into *both* categories!

Two people can have an identical experience and yet, because of their individual emotional reaction or belief system, may interpret the experience in totally divergent ways. Also, many UFO encounters contain both positive and negative elements, making it very difficult to define the experience as either wholly positive or negative.

Maryann is a case in point. Maryann lives alone with her young daughter in a condominium complex in a crowded suburb of Carpinteria, California. She works as a waitress and, in most respects, lives a normal life—normal, that is, except for one small feature: she seems to be in contact with an extraterrestrial.

The alien is a "small gray" alien typically associated with traumatic abductions. However, in this case, no abductions seem to have occurred. On the contrary, instead of abducting Maryann, this alien arrives as a friendly visitor. Even more unusual is that, to Maryann's great surprise, she's able to communicate with the visitor via automatic writing. So began her relationship with an alien named "Kevin."

Actually, Maryann's experiences with UFOs go much further back. She has had at least three separate UFO sightings earlier in her life, the first occurring in 1978 in Santa Barbara, California. The sun had just set, and Maryann and her boyfriend, Warren, were driving on Foothill Boulevard, a major city street. Suddenly, something very strange occurred, something so strange that it caused a police officer driving in the opposite direction to immediately drift out of his lane and nearly collide into Maryann and Warren head-on!

Maryann recalled what happened. "It was kind of dark. We were cruising along, and all of a sudden, one half of the sky lit up. I'm talking one half, like it was split down the middle. On the right-hand side toward the mountains, it was normal dusk-type day, and the left-hand side was just dead-black dark. And we both look up in the sky, and we say, 'What the hell's going on?' Because, we know that Vandenburg [Air Force Base] is here and they set off Minuteman missiles all the time. And we thought that that's what it was. And we're kind of cruising along, not paying much attention to the road, and we look up, and there's a sheriff coming at us in our lane, looking up. He didn't even know that he had veered over into our lane. And there was another car behind us. We all three pulled over and we get out of the car and we say, 'What the f— was that?'

The four people discussed briefly what they saw. None of them could identify what they had seen. It just appeared to be a bright light that covered a good portion of the sky. Maryann and Warren still favored the missile explanation, that is, until they returned home.

"But then . . . we got home." Maryann recalled. "And we had a roommate who had a telescope and had observed this whole thing, and it came up out of the ocean. It was a ship and it came up out of the ocean. We got home and we thought there was nobody home, and then we heard somebody walking around the balcony upstairs. He was walking around and he was in a daze. He was going, 'God, I can't believe that!'

"I said, 'Did that have anything to do with half the sky lighting up?'

"And he said, 'God, it was incredible.' And he told us all about this thing that came up out of the ocean and he tracked it with his telescope. And he said it moved so fast, it was unbelievable—obviously nothing from this earth. He just happened to be there. He was taking a class in astronomy and was setting up his telescope and happened to observe this. So that was the first sighting I ever saw."

Like many UFO witnesses, Maryann assumed that after this one sighting, her experiences were over. For most witnesses, this would be true. About one year later, in the summer of 1979, Maryann was to have another dramatic UFO sighting.

On this occasion, she and her boyfriend were driving across the United States. They were in Utah, in an isolated part of the state. Around 4:00 A.M. Maryann and Warren saw a strange light that appeared to be pacing their car.

Maryann remembered, "I looked out the window and I said, 'Warren, what the hell is that out there?' What it looked like to me was a railroad signal. I said, 'What is that?'

"He said, 'Well, it's a railroad signal.'

"And I said, 'Well, if it's a railroad signal, how come it's pacing us? How come every time I look out my window, it's there? We should have passed it twenty miles down the road.' It was green and glowing quite brightly."

They watched the light and realized that it could not be stationary. Whatever it was, it kept right up with them, even though they were driving at around seventy miles per hour. They began to get a little nervous because the object not only kept pace with them, but it showed no signs of leaving.

"It was a good distance, maybe six hundred, seven hundred yards, a half a mile maybe. It didn't look very big because it was so far off in the distance. It was pretty big. It wasn't little. It was bigger than a Volkswagen. And it stayed with us. But it was low to the ground. It stayed with us probably about a hundred miles. And then it just vanished. It took off straight up. It didn't take off; it didn't just fly off. It just went from basically going along the horizon and then a complete ninety-degree turn and then straight up. Nothing that we make can do that."

After the unexplained light left, both of them were a little relieved. Try as they might, they simply could not explain it. Because of the way it left, both were convinced that they had seen something very unusual.

Maryann's third experience occurred nearly nine years later, back in Santa Barbara. Again, there were multiple witnesses to the sighting. It was the summer of 1988. "The last time I saw something was camping up in Santa Barbara, back in the hills. . . . We were all sitting around and it was pretty dark. And we observed three of these same green, glowing 'odd-ball thingies.' They were weird and hovering, and doing all kinds of bizarre maneuvers. They would go up, they would go down. They were close enough that you know they're not stars. They were probably about a mile off, but they were above the mountains."

It was the motion of the objects that most impressed Maryann and her friends. "Very precise cutting motions. They didn't move smoothly. They moved, and then they stopped. And then they would move in another direction and then stop . . . move in another direction and then stop . . . move in another direction and stop. Then they moved off. There were three of them. They were all moving independent of one another. One would go and then stop. One would go slightly off the left and then stop. Then the other would go way to the right and then stop. And no noise from any of these encounters."

The four campers watched the lights for about twenty minutes, at which point the lights disappeared. Again, nobody could come up with any satisfactory explanation for them.

After the third sighting, Marianne was left with a strengthened belief in the existence of UFOs. Nothing, however, could have prepared her for the experience she would have four years later, one evening in October 1992.

It all began when Maryann returned home from work. She had just finished dinner, and was relaxing, drinking a glass of wine and watching television. On that particular night, the program *Unsolved Mysteries* was airing, so Maryann decided to watch it. She had no idea what was in store, or she probably would have turned off the TV and gone straight to bed. But it was too late. She quickly became intrigued by a particular segment of the program that focussed on a series of UFO sightings in Hudson Valley, New York. Maryann was watching a policewoman tell of her close encounter with a silent UFO, when she suddenly became aware that there was a presence in the room. Although she couldn't actually see anybody, she was convinced that something was there. She became frightened and called up a friend and told her to come over quickly. That's when things began to go from strange to truly bizarre.

"All of a sudden," Maryann remembered, "I started to not hear anything, but recognize that there was another presence around. So I called Suzy up, because I was kind of scared, and she came over and started asking me some questions. And I started writing with my left hand."

Maryann didn't know it at the time, but she experienced a phenomenon known as automatic writing. In fact, Maryann was actually "channeling." Although she didn't exactly understand what was happening, she knew she was in contact with something. She was not left-handed, and yet, something was moving her left hand, and writing down the answers to numerous questions. She knew it wasn't her own subconscious because, in her mind, she could see exactly who was responsible; it certainly wasn't her—in fact, it wasn't even human.

Maryann's mind was quickly flooded with information. She recalled, "I knew exactly what his name was. He popped right up and said his name was Kevin, which I thought was kind of bizarre. This benign name. Not 'Nordinork' or something weird like that, but Kevin!"

Although Maryann couldn't see Kevin with her physical eyes, she had a very clear picture of him in her mind. "He's hairless. He's pale. He's short. He's very thin. He's vaguely human—I mean, more than vaguely; he's got two legs, two arms, two eyes, a nose, a mouth, no lips."

When asked to describe the eyes, Maryann gave a very common description often attributed to gray-type aliens. "They're almond-shaped and they're dark, and there are no pupils." Maryann was also able to see Kevin's body, and was surprised to see that he wore no clothes at all. "He doesn't wear anything, but it's kind of an asexual body. You can't tell who the male, or the female, is."

At first Maryann could see the alleged alien, but not talk to him. All the communication was through automatic writing. Maryann's friend, Suzy, would ask a question, and Maryann's hand would scribble out the answer. Very quickly, her at-first illegible writing began to improve. "I do it all left-handed, and I don't write left-handed. I can't write left-handed at any other time."

Maryann reports that she feels "slightly dissociated" when she does the writing, which is a typical symptom of channeling. She definitely feels like she is not controlling her arm. She says simply, "I feel separate." Her hand would also twitch and jerk around of its own accord. "Well, I do weird little things with it, before I start to write. It starts to . . . like . . . move, not back and forth, but just more of a shaking motion. It's, like, 'incoming.' That's what it feels like, 'incoming.'"

As Maryann began communicating in earnest, her fear evaporated, and she actually began to telepathically hear the answers in her mind, before they were written. "Suzy will ask me a question, like, 'What do they do?' And it'll just kind of come to me. 'Well, this is what they do.'" It was then that she began to learn more about Kevin, where he comes from, and why he was communicating with her. "He just said his name is Kevin. He's very interested in our interest in him and his race. He calls it a race. It's a race. He doesn't call it any particular race. He doesn't say, 'Kevin Martian.' Just that they've been here for a long, long, long, long, long, long, long time. Longer than we have, from what I understand."

The flood of information continued. Often, Maryann and Suzy didn't even have to ask any questions. Kevin just offered the information. "They're vastly interested in us. They're almost more interested in us than we are in them. They're fascinated by us. They don't think the same way we do."

It wasn't long before Maryann found out where Kevin lived—a place one would least expect. "They live in the ocean, underwater. In the water, literally . . . their ships are underwater. They're very benign. They've got no nuclear . . . warheads [or] this kind of stuff. They're benign. They're a benign race. They live in our oceans. They live in all the oceans. He didn't particular say that they live in earth oceans. He said, 'We live in oceans.'"

Many channelers and contactees are given prophecies of future events, often of upcoming catastrophes. Often the prophecies do not come true. Maryann's case is no exception. Kevin warned her that an earthquake of a magnitude greater than eight points on the Richter scale would hit Los Angeles in December 1995. Fortunately this did not occur. As Maryann recalled, "He was telling me something about earthquakes . . . Suzy's got it all written down . . . he didn't predict anything else. He just said we're in for some type of big natural disaster. I get the impression, thinking back to what he talks to me about, is that they're almost here to warn us. Not of an impending doom type of thing like the world's going to blow up, but they're not here to hurt. They're here to observe . . ."

The theme of global catastrophes turns up often in UFO accounts. The aliens seem to be convinced that our planet is heading towards natural disasters unparalleled in modern history. Although many of these prophecies have failed to materialize, this is not always the case. I worked closely with one abductee whose encounter occurred the night before the devastating quake that struck Northridge, California, causing nearly fifty deaths and millions of dollars in property damage. In her case, the aliens also warned her of a catastrophic event that would occur on Jupiter. This was months before comet Shoemaker-Levy struck the giant planet, having a much greater impact on Jupiter than most scientists had predicted.

Maryann isn't sure why the aliens contacted her and not someone else, but she feels that the relationship is very personal. "I get the impression that I am not the only one he talks to. In fact, I think that it's like a job for them. That's kind of the impression I got, is they kind of probe people, different people. It's like his job is a probe to find people who are receptive."

Maryann was also given more information of a somewhat shocking nature. Kevin told her that his race is much more numerous than all of humanity. "Lots and lots and lots. This is not just five or ten or twenty ships roaming around. We're talking, from what I get from him, millions and millions of these people. And they've existed before we recorded time and history."

Sometimes Maryann began to question whether or not this information was coming from her imagination, but after thinking about it for a long time, she no longer questions herself. "I don't know whether or not he's impressed this on me . . . well, I'm sure he has because how would I know all this stuff? That's the understanding I have. They have jobs like everybody has jobs down here. His job is to find people who are receptive enough that he can talk to. And he was really worried about whether or not I was really scared."

Maryann was able to communicate at length with Kevin on two separate occasions. Much of the above information was received during the second communication, which began with Maryann suddenly sensing Kevin's presence. There was another occasion when Maryann was talking on the phone with Suzy, and Kevin showed up with a personal message for Suzy. On another occasion, Suzy just happened to bring up the name of a well-known UFO researcher, and Kevin became extremely angry. Evidently, he did not agree with this particular UFO researcher and the work he is doing in the UFO field. However, Maryann feels that Kevin is definitely a friendly alien. "I'm certainly not afraid of him."

Kevin has not made any additional appearance, but Maryann feels that she could probably call Kevin quite easily. She is eager to learn more about him. For example, he never even gave his last name, and she suspects that the name Kevin was used by him simply to make her less afraid.

Maryann knows that automatic writing can be used for communicating with spirits, but ironically, the idea of talking to ghosts scares her more than talking with aliens. She simply said, "I don't want to talk with spirits . . . I'm not into that."

Unfortunately for Maryann, her ability to channel makes her very receptive to spirit communication.

This fact was proved to Maryann when a close friend of hers was murdered. Maryann became involved in a complicated trial afterwards. It was then that she began sensing her friend's spirit. She believes that she was able to talk to the spirit of her friend on at least two separate occasions.

Maryann has no plans to channel Kevin professionally, and has told only a few people about her experiences. She seeks no publicity. She does not feel a need to contact Kevin, nor does she feel a need to stop the contacts. She didn't initiate it, so she is comfortable to let things evolve on their own.

Encounters with aliens take many different forms. Some people are taken physically into craft by gray-type aliens, while others are contacted telepathically. Sometimes the experience is scary, sometimes it is not. Maryann's case does have many features in common with other accounts, including gray-type aliens, the telepathic communication, the warnings of global catastrophes, and other smaller details. Yet it also has obviously unique features that place it on the extreme end of the bell curve. However, as no mysteries can be solved by eliminating information, I have chosen to include her account.

Fortunately for Maryann, her experience was not traumatic. In fact, she likes Kevin. "He's pretty nice. He's pretty friendly."

Alien in the Bedroom

Most cases involving very close encounters with extraterrestrials follow certain common patterns, including missing time, beams of light that levitate the abductee, accounts of telepathy, similar descriptions of alien lifeforms wearing tight jumpsuits. Even UFO interiors seem remarkably alike with their rounded walls, examination rooms, indirect lighting, and advanced technological instruments.

Despite these obvious patterns, each case is unique and almost always presents new details never reported before. Each case provides another piece of the puzzle that is the UFO phenomenon.

In 1967, Paul Nelson was twelve years old when his parents decided to take him and his childhood friend, Michael Stein (both names were changed at the witnesses' request), to Catalina Island off the coast of southern California. It was a vacation that would ultimately change the direction of Paul's life.

At his age, Paul had no conception of UFOs. Even when he experienced a bizarre episode of missing time, he didn't connect it to the UFO phenomenon until much later. It all began when he and Michael bought some new comic books. Excited about reading them, they headed back to Paul's father's boat, which was docked in Avalon Harbor. That's when something very strange occurred.

Paul remembered it clearly. "I was on my dad's boat in the lower cabin area with my friend, Michael Stein. We just got back from Avalon on our little dinghy with our comic books, very excited about reading them. It was just after dark, far away from sleep time. And we sat down, got our comic books open, and then instantly we were unconscious. The next thing we realize, it was morning. And both of us had no idea how we had lost consciousness or what happened that evening. My parents said that they came back some time after midnight and found us asleep at that time. So it was quite anomalous that both of us would have this happen at the same time."

The next morning, both Paul and Michael knew that something unusual had occurred. It seemed impossible to them that they had just suddenly fallen asleep. Neither had been the least bit tired. It was long before bedtime. And both were eager to read their new comic books. None of it made any sense. The next morning, Paul asked his parents, "What happened to us? We were sitting there and had just opened our comic books."

His parents could only speculate that they had fallen asleep. But Paul knew this wasn't the case. It was much more like suddenly becoming unconscious. It was as if a period of time was simply missing. He knew that it was unusual, but he had no explanation to account for it. It was a mystery that would gnaw at him for years to come.

However, a mere two or three weeks later, Paul was back at his parents' home in the dense suburb of Sherman Oaks, California. He was alone in the house. All the doors were locked, and he was playing in his bedroom. Suddenly, there was somebody at the door to his bedroom. His first impression was that an intruder had somehow gotten into the house. But whoever was at the door was not behaving like an intruder would behave. In fact, the whole situation quickly became very strange.

As Paul recalled, "I was home alone and I had an experience where the door was rattling as if there was somebody at the door. And I could hear footsteps outside the door. I thought there was an intruder. I kind of wondered where I got the gumption, but I went to the door and opened it and looked outside. And there was a shadow . . . on the hallway about ten feet from the door. And there were footsteps, but it was more like animal footsteps, of little feet moving quickly along the entry hall floor. I assumed that a dog had gotten in, but I couldn't imagine how it could reach for the doorknob or rattle the doorknob.

"The shadow looked like a small little being actually, to me, which didn't make any sense. And it appeared that there were two legs in the shadow. So I was very confused at the time, and I didn't equate it with UFOs. I chased after the shadow, turned the corner, and there was nothing there. And I should have been able to reach whatever was there. I checked all the doors; I checked for holes in the wall—nothing. There was no way for an animal to exit the house, or no place to hide. I checked the whole house. Nothing was there."

After searching the house for an intruder and not finding any, Paul could only speculate and wonder. There seemed to be no explanation—he was absolutely sure that he had heard the door rattling and the sound of tiny footsteps pattering across the hallway, and was equally certain that he had seen the shadow of a small figure. Even though the shadow seemed to have two legs, he didn't equate it with a person. It simply was not possible that a child had gotten into the house with all the doors locked. To further compound the mystery, when Paul turned the corner to the hallway, nobody was there. It was all very strange to him. When his parents came home, Paul told them what happened and that there must have been an animal that had somehow gotten into the house. His parents' response was a predictable "What?"

They, too, had no explanation. At the time, Paul didn't connect it to the Catalina incident. He assumed that there was a logical explanation to how an animal had gotten in and out of the house, and never mind that it turned the doorknob and cast a humanoid-shaped shadow on the wall. He simply filed the memory in the back of his mind for future reference. It wasn't long, however, before little clues began to emerge in his consciousness that something bizarre had indeed happened.

The first clue took the form of a strange and vivid dream shortly following the bedroom encounter. "I had a strange dream," Paul said. "There was a strange light outside my window, which I made the assumption was a fire in the neighborhood. But there wasn't, now that I think about it." It wasn't until recently, however, that Paul made any connections to the dream, and what had happened to him.

Another aftereffect of the events at Catalina Island and Sherman Oaks was a sudden and profound interest in the subject of UFOs. "Soon after that I started having an interest in extraterrestrial discussion. At that time I read the Barney and Betty Hill story, *Interrupted Journey,* and kept an interest in this. These events, when I was twelve, were occurring in 1967. In 1968 my interest continued. And then in 1969, when the Condon Commission came out saying that there was no truth to the phenomenon, I dropped it."

For years following the incidents, Paul would occasionally think about what happened and wonder. But he left it at that. It was simply a mystery he couldn't understand.

Later on, as a teenager, while thinking about the Catalina Island incident, he hit upon a wild theory that he thought might explain what happened in Avalon Harbor. He quickly told his parents to see if they could verify his theory. "I had the assumption later on in my teenage years that maybe I had been gassed by leaking propane, something like that, and had been knocked out with Michael. But then I asked my parents about it, and they said, 'No, there was no leaking propane. Where did you get that idea?'" So as quickly as he came up with the theory, he threw it away. There was also the fact that they never remembered smelling any propane gas, which does have a distinct and powerful odor.

Years went by, and Paul grew into an adult. He went to medical school, where he met his wife, also a medical student. They both became doctors, married, had two children and lived the American Dream in their modest suburban home, not far from where he had grown up.

Then, in 1992, his interest in the UFOs was suddenly sparked by a sighting of an anomalous, glowing object over the desert. Before he knew it, he was buying all the books he could find and voraciously reading all the materials available on the subject. He joined several UFO study groups and became more and more deeply involved in the UFO community. His wife, too, sighted a disk-like object hovering over Topanga Canyon near their home, and she also developed an interest in the subject.

Still, Paul had no idea why his interest in the subject bordered on obsession. It just seemed fascinating to him. He didn't feel as though he was personally involved. At this time, he only rarely thought about the mysterious events of his childhood.

Then, one day while he was reading a book about missing time experiences, he suddenly remembered that he also had once experienced missing time. This eventually led him to seek out a hypnotherapist to recover any memories that may have been blocked out. He located a hypnotherapist with considerable knowledge of the subject matter, and who had performed numerous regressions of UFO abductees. Under hypnosis, he relived an abduction story that even today he has difficulty believing actually happened to him.

Regarding his first experience with missing time, Paul recalled, "I was reading the literature about the events in childhood with missing time, and I thought . . . 'Well, gee, this sounds like something could have happened.' So under regression, I apparently—and there's no way I know for sure that the regression is accessing memory rather than accessing imagination, but this is what my imagination or memory presented—that I was taken into a round-walled room. It seemed to me more underground than it did onboard a ship. The walls had kind of a rock-like facet to them. And I was on a table. But my memory at this point involved only being kind of kept waiting while these beings worked on my friend, Michael. I was just kind of in an anteroom while the real goings-on were with Michael. I was just the target of opportunity, I guess.

"There were some machines on the walls. The beings weren't the typical grays, they were more the 'Praying Mantis' type as I later understood the phenotype. The eyes were slightly bigger than what is seen in the typical small gray, and a little more insectoid-like. . . . I'm trying to remember back to the regression. They wore tight-fitting uniforms, I believe. There was even a color to them, but I can't remember what the color was . . . tight-fitting jumpsuit-like things as I remember. I think there was one in that bunch that had a tunic-type thing, more looser fitting over it. I couldn't tell how tall they were exactly because they were over me and I was on my back on the table. So I couldn't give you the exact height. They didn't look particularly tall though. And one of them had his hand on my leg, and one came in through the door. I could see beyond that into the hallway. I couldn't really see very much. And one of them said in my mind, 'Wait here,' or 'Wait.' . . . There were two that I remember at this point. I think there was a third one on the wall handling the console. There was one touching my leg, one came in the door and one on the console. And then that's the last I remembered about that encounter, that so-called event if it really was an event."

Paul was unable to recall how he was apparently taken onboard or returned. Nor did he recall seeing Michael onboard. "I had the impression that he was in another room and I was waiting for him to get done . . . [I was] just lying there, not having anything done to me, which gave me the impression that I wasn't the actual target. I was just there waiting for Michael and they were doing something with him."

Paul also felt a bit ambiguous about his recall under hypnosis and wondered if his imagination was simply concocting a story to fill in the blanks. What's interesting about his recall is that Paul had previously read a considerable amount of material concerning onboard UFO experiences. In one sense, this could be construed as a "contamination factor," meaning that his own recall could have been pieced together from the accounts of others. Interestingly however, Paul's recall of the events contained several unique and totally unexpected details not usually found in mainstream abduction accounts. This lends credence to the theory that his recall of the events that occurred during the missing-time segment is valid.

One detail that surprised him was his memory of being underground rather than onboard a ship. "Yeah," Paul remembered. "Rock-like walls rather than metallic craft-type walls. It gave the impression that I was in a cavern [rather] than in a ship . . . It was more of an underground feeling, that's true. That is a little anomalous . . . guessing now, it was fifteen feet from the table to the wall, so maybe a thirty-foot radius in all."

Another detail that surprised him was the computer-like instruments, which seemed less extraterrestrial in design than he would have otherwise expected. "The machines looked like typical military-type computer consoles rather than alien-looking machines . . . there were lights and button. Well, I don't know if they were buttons, but areas that seemed to be for pushing. Colored lights—I can't remember what color off the top of my head."

Still another detail that he was not expecting was the appearance of the beings. In most of the cases he had read, the grays figured predominantly, and prior to his regression, that is truly what he expected to see. As he said, what he saw really surprised him. "Yeah, that the beings weren't the typical grays. They were more— they looked a little—well, at this point, I mean, maybe I knew about 'Praying Mantis,' but they looked more like that than the typical grays. They were slightly more insectoid-looking than the grays."

After recalling the first incident, the hypnotherapist quickly regressed him to the next incident in Paul's home. Paul was again surprised by his recall of the events. "The second time . . . I was the target in this case. I was taken onboard. I don't remember having any samples taken. As memory or imagination serves, I don't remember being particularly scared about the whole thing. In fact, I was a little intrigued by it. And I don't remember anything painful occurring . . . the second one was more of a craft. It was more of a craft-type room. Although I remembered a light over me at one point . . . I don't think I saw the walls of that room. I saw . . . the light and the beings over me."

Paul doesn't recall any bizarre experiments being performed on him, nor really much activity by the beings at all. "Not a whole heck of a lot. I think they were done by that time. If they were doing anything, they were probably done by the time I remember. I couldn't tell you."

On this occasion, Paul actually remembered the beings, which appeared to be the same ones as before, coming into the house and carrying him into the ship.

"I can't remember the exact details, but I remember them being in the room, and then I'm onboard the ship, and then they're back in the room making sure I'm okay, and then exiting out the door, after which I chased them."

Unlike many abductees, Paul did not find the experience frightening. Perhaps it was because he had already done so much reading on the subject and had some foreknowledge about what might occur. Or perhaps it was because there was nothing hideous about the experience. "No, neither experience was scary. It was more intriguing. If anybody were to abduct me, I would find it totally fascinating. I mean, they would really have to do something extremely bad for me to get scared at this point. I was pretty intrigued by the whole concept. So I don't remember being scared, no."

After going under hypnosis, Paul admits that he was a little disappointed. Like many abductees, he discovered that hypnosis is not exactly like experiencing an event as it occurs. In some ways he almost feels like he "paid the fee" and "got the story" he was looking for. On the other hand, he has every reason to believe that the events occurred exactly as he remembered them under hypnosis.

Because of his ambiguous feelings about his recall, he conducted a long search for his childhood friend, with whom he had since lost contact. Unfortunately he was unable to locate him even by using an Internet search on his friend's name, which is not a very common name. So any hopes of verifying his story with corroboration from Michael have been put on hold.

Again, he was left with an enduring mystery about what really happened. "Now, I'm not saying that these events [recalled under hypnosis] really occurred. The two events in Catalina and Sherman Oaks really did happen to me. There was honest-to-God missing time witnessed by my friend who had missing time also. And then the second event in Sherman Oaks actually did happen. I remember, it was a very vivid event in my memory. It was always puzzling to me how that could happen. The events—I still have to explain those events, and I haven't been able to explain them in any other way at this point. Very strange consciously remembered events, and certainly from what I know now about missing time and anomalous phenomena, I think it's very possible."

After the hypnotic regression, Paul continued to have a deep interest in UFOs. However, he is no longer obsessed with the subject. He only occasionally meets with UFO groups, just enough to keep up with any new developments in the field. He seeks no publicity at all, preferring to remain anonymous, and has told very few people about his experiences.

Today, he continues to live his life, comfortable with the possibility that he may or may not have been abducted by aliens.

A Crash Course in UFOs

The process of becoming aware that you are an abductee can be instantaneous, or it may take years. Invariably, however, the abductee is shocked to discover that he or she has been having contact for some time, without being aware of it. Each person goes through his or her own process of denial or acceptance. Each person develops unique ways of adapting and trying to deal with the experience.

For Melinda Leslie, an office and store manager, a series of remarkable coincidences led her to the incredible discovery that she had been experiencing contacts with extraterrestrials. In a matter of two years, Melinda went from living as a UFO skeptic, to knowing that she has had dozens of contacts with extraterrestrials, spanning from her early childhood to the present day. For Melinda, the whole ordeal began with a UFO sighting in 1987, in Sedona, Arizona. At the time, she was very skeptical of UFOs. "I really didn't have an interest in the subject," she said. "In fact, I even had an aversion to it. I was never a sci-fi fan or anything like that."

Then Melinda had her first sighting. At the time, she and her friends were having a "meditational experience." No one was prepared for what would happen next. Melinda recalled, "Someone received a message that if we went outside we would see a UFO. We went outside . . . it was late in the afternoon. There was a group of twenty or thirty of us. We went outside and sure enough, someone said, 'Oh, look!' . . . And we saw three orange lights flying in formation. There was blue sky behind them, so it was three separate objects that were moving about erratically in the sky and keeping the same formation while they moved about. This went on for about—it seemed like a couple of minutes, but it may have been a minute . . . it wasn't that long, maybe thirty seconds, but it was enough that we were discussing it when we were seeing it. It moved around and then all of a sudden just shot off really fast. And they kept in this exact formation."

The group's reaction to the sighting was also unusual. As we have previously seen, in many cases where groups of people are involved, the reaction to the event, ironically, can be subdued. This was true in this case. "It wasn't a big deal," Melinda recalled. "It was incredible and amazing, but it was kind of like it wasn't a big deal."

Melinda's first sighting failed to spark in her any real interest in the subject. She rarely thought about it, and only talked about it when she ran into her friends in Arizona. Then, two years later, a coworker of Melinda's encouraged her to listen to a radio broadcast called Billy Goodman's *The Happening Radio Program*. Her coworker had listened to the show, which at the time focussed on the breaking story of Area 51. Melinda's coworker was impressed by the reports of UFO sightings at Area 51, and again encouraged Melinda to at least listen to the show.

Although Melinda wasn't really interested, she listened to the program. During the program, it was announced that one could actually visit the area outside Area 51, and maybe have a UFO sighting. Melinda's coworker asked Melinda if she wanted to go. They had previously gone on desert camping trips before, and the idea seemed a little intriguing, but Melinda had prior commitments. Not only did she have to work on the day the trip was being planned, but she also had to help her brother with a party he was having. Then, as if by fate, another coworker asked Melinda to switch workshifts with her, and her brother called to say that he didn't really need her help after all. So Melinda and two friends piled into a rental car and headed off to Area 51 in the vast desert northwest of Las Vegas, and where Nellis Air Force Base is also located.

The drive took all day and they arrived at around 10:30 P.M. Melinda wasn't sure what to expect, but it was nothing at all like what actually happened. "The radio station had taken a couple of busloads of people out there. And they had advertised it heavily on the radio. Well, there were tons of people there. There were two full busloads, they had a bunch of people in cars. My guess is that there were eighty people there or more. People were starting to leave because they had been there all night at this point . . . We stopped everyone, we asked, 'Did you see anything?' 'Yeah, we had three sightings.'

"We thought, 'What? Oh, my God! That's incredible!' When we went out there, we didn't expect to see anything. We thought we were going out there with a bunch of people who were going to carry on and meditate and hold hands. And that's not the kind of crowd it was at all. It was amateur astronomers, conspiracy buffs, military experts . . . this wasn't the kind of crowd we expected. And a lot of older folks because the people that came on the bus from Vegas were predominantly older people.

"This wasn't what we had expected. Well, everyone ended up leaving except for a group of us. It was between 11:00 P.M. and 3:00 A.M. The crowd had dwindled down to about twenty people who were still there. And about the twenty of us who had been there agreed that we had approximately . . . about fifteen sightings that we had all seen."

The sightings involved mostly anomalous lights that maneuvered in patterns the observers knew out-performed any plane, helicopter, or conventional air-craft. "That was pretty amazing." Melinda recalled. "I didn't realize it at the time, but something about that changed my belief system. First of all, *they* existed. I've seen them with my own eyes. What I've seen defies gravity and science and aerodynamics and physics as I know it. It was pretty amazing stuff.

"Secondly, to the degree that there were these white Bronco jeeps cruising over the hill constantly, and helicopters in the air, they were not being shot at, or chased after, or flown after . . . and this was a known military base. Okay, so first off, they exist. Second, the government knows about it because here they are fully out there at the same time. And this is a known mili-tary base, so I figured, 'Okay, well they know about it, so they're lying.'

"And third, not only do they know about it and they're lying, but this goes on regularly. These things are flying in and out of here on a regular basis. Wait a second, that's interaction. That goes beyond the fact that they just know something. That's the fact that they're in bed with them.

"So I had three major shifts in consciousness at once, which was they exist, there's a cover-up, and there's involvement. And it was pretty wild, in one night. Well, we got so excited by what we had seen, we couldn't wait to go back out there again."

Melinda didn't know it at the time, but this visit marked not only a shift in her consciousness about the existence of UFOs, but the beginning of her realization that she was having contact with them. Two weeks later she and her friends again drove out to Area 51. "We even rearranged and canceled plans to do it. We went out there again. So did most of the people who were out there that night with us . . . so two weeks later we went out all the way to Nevada again, and had more sightings. And then we went back about a month later. We went back again . . . so we had more sightings then."

By this time, Melinda's belief system had become totally transformed. She was no longer the disinterested skeptic she used to be. She was intrigued with the whole subject. Also around this time Melinda had a series of mysterious dreams about a few puzzling events in her childhood. These were her first real clues that she may have a very personal involvement with the UFO phenomenon.

As Melinda remembered, "Well, in the midst of these three trips out there, I started having dreams at night of being a little kid . . . this one dream for instance. I went out to play, outside in the desert. My grandmother had a house in Yucca Valley [California].

She had a little homestead out in the middle of nowhere really. There was nothing around. She had one neighbor who was a couple of hundred yards away. That was the closest neighbor. And we would go out there all the time for holidays . . . and I had one dream about being out there as a kid, going out there and playing one afternoon. And I remember thinking it got dark really quick, so I came back home. I was scared because it was dark. I found my way back home and everyone was really mad. 'Where have you been?! We've been looking all over for you. We called the neighbors! We called the sheriff! Where have you been?'

"Apparently, I had been [missing] . . . And I didn't think I had been gone that long. I was just out playing, and I remember it suddenly got dark. And as a kid you don't have a lot of judgment of time, but I don't remember thinking it was that long. And they said, 'We have been looking for you all night. Where have you been?'

"I said, 'I was just out playing.' I was like five and didn't know. So suddenly, I'm having this dream surface about this thing that *really happened* to me as a kid. And I thought, 'Why am I dreaming about that?'"

At the same time that Melinda was becoming increasingly interested in UFOs, she had more dreams of events that had actually happened to her as a child. And each of these dreams uncovered another clue that she was personally involved with UFOs.

Her next dream was even more revealing. "Then I realized that I had missing time. It was a dream about a real childhood experience where I thought I went out to play for an hour or two, and it was well into the evening. So I realized, 'There's that.'

"And then I had another dream surface of being a little kid, and being put down for a nap, again at my grandmother's house in Yucca Valley, and everyone going off and doing something. All the older kids. I'm the youngest. And one of the adults would stay there to stay and watch me, and I was put down for my afternoon nap. And I remember being awoken from this nap by what I thought were little kids at the bedroom window wanting me to come out and play with them. And I think I went out the front door . . . and I have a vague memory of it being my mom who stayed behind and that she had fallen asleep, and I didn't want to awaken her or whatever, and I went outside to play with these kids. It's all a very vague memory, but I remember. I had this dream about these kids coming to the window and waking me up from a nap and then I went out and played with them. And then I realized I'm having that dream as well as a few other dreams that were similar. And I thought, 'Now why am I suddenly having all these dreams about being a kid out in Yucca Valley?'

"[There were] some other related things. Another time, another thing that happened with the whole family. We ran out of gas while driving out there once. And we were out in the middle of nowhere. And my brother went to go get help. And I had that dream too, and I thought, why is that surfacing? So these things were coming up. Those dreams were actually happening before the third trip out there."

During her third trip out to Area 51, Melinda brought up the subject to her friends. She said, "You know, guys, I've been having these weird dreams."

They said, "Oh, my God. It sounds like you're having experiences."

Melinda's response was, "No, no, these are just dreams."

They said, "Listen to what you're saying."

Melinda still wasn't convinced. A few weeks later, she listened to a radio program about an abductee who recounted her experiences. As Melinda listened to the woman's story, she became unaccountably upset, and actually called up the station and expressed her skepticism of the case. As Melinda recalled, "What she was saying was upsetting me . . . At the time I had no idea that anything was going on, but what she was saying was upsetting me and I was arguing with her about it."

Later, Melinda had the opportunity to actually meet the abductee featured on the program. They met at a coffee shop. After talking for awhile, Melinda shared her peculiar dreams. The abductee flatly stated, "So, you've had this happen."

Melinda replied, "No, I haven't."

The woman said, "We just spent, like, an hour sitting here . . . talking about it, and you're telling me about your experiences."

Melinda said, "No, no, no. I'm talking about things that happened to me as a kid."

The woman replied, "Listen to what you're saying."

Melinda was shocked. "I was like, 'Whoa!' And that really bugged me. I was like, 'Oh, my God. Am I having this happen? What's going on?'"

Melinda went home, anxiously wondering, could she have had UFO experiences in her childhood? Little did she know it, but she was about to have another, only now she was an adult.

Melinda went to sleep that night, only to awaken the next morning to her radio making very strange noises. "I woke up in the morning," she recalled. "And my radio was making popping and clicking noises. I thought maybe I left it on. So I checked it and it was off. But it was still doing it."

Melinda didn't think much of it until she went to get ready for work. "So I get in the shower and I start to shave my legs, and I find a bruise on one ankle. Okay, no big deal. I'm shaving more, 'Oh, look, there's another bruise. How did I get those?' And there were these two on either side of my left ankle. And there was one by my left knee—a square outline and two holes in the middle of it. And it was swollen. I squeezed it with my fingers and those two holes were fresh. When I squeezed it really good, it would bleed, like two large needles right next to each other with a square outline around it. Then I went up, and there were some more bruises. And then the other ankle had the same two bruises on either side that the left ankle had. Well, I started to slowly come unglued in the shower. 'Oh, my God! . . . I had better come to the realization that something had happened to me.' I was very, very upset.

"I went to work that morning, wore sheer black nylons. A woman I worked with was standing about ten feet away from me. And she was staring at my legs. When I realized she was, she said, 'Oh, I'm sorry. Actually, I don't mean to be staring at you. I was just concerned.'

"I said, 'What do you mean?'

"She said, "Did you get in a fight with a boyfriend or something?'

"I said, 'No, I'm not seeing anybody right now.'

"She said, 'Oh, you've got some bruises on your legs.'

"I said, 'They're not that bad. I didn't think anybody would notice.'

"She said, 'Well, how did you get them?'

"I said, "I don't know.'

"She said, 'Did you fall out of bed?'

"I said, 'No.'

"She walked up to me. 'Well, that one looks like a

spider bite,' she pointed to the one by my knee. You could tell it was a little bit swollen."

Melinda became concerned all over again. "It was obviously too big to be a spider bite . . . I started to realize maybe something was happening."

A few months later, Melinda had another bizarre experience. She had just finished an intense phone conversation with a friend, and was meditating to clear her mind before she went to bed. "It's just a visualization exercise and that's it. It takes maybe two minutes. I did it and I turned to turn off my light next to me. And as I went to reach for the light, I glanced down at the alarm clock and I did this double-take. It was two and a half hours later from when I had just seen it. And I knew exactly what time it was. It was 11:40 because I remember I was getting to bed late. And here it was, like 2:30 in the morning. It was 2:30, and I'm going, 'What?! I just sat on my bed." I knew exactly what time it was, and now it was two and a half hours later. There was no way I was sitting on my bed for two and a half hours. Absolutely no way. No way. And I knew then that I had had missing time."

Melinda became immediately alarmed, but quickly calmed down to try and think about what had just happened. She cleared her mind and let herself think back to where the time went. Suddenly, a strange image entered her mind. "The first thing that came to my mind was a visual image of three grays that were slightly varied in height . . . and they were standing next to my bed and reaching for me. And this is a long story, but they had this silver blanket-like thing in their hands. They were reaching for me with this blanket-like thing like they were going to lay it on me or something. And I couldn't get that visual image out of my head."

By now, Melinda was more than a little upset. She knew now that something scary and unusual was happening to her. "I was crying. I was so upset. It was three o'clock in the morning now, and I was sitting in bed, just a wreck. I had to wake up at seven to go to work."

Melinda did her best to forget the experience, relax, and go to sleep. She went to work the next day, and just tried to push the experience out of her mind. She was successful for two days, until her roommate, who was living in the townhouse, revealed some startling new information. She approached Melinda and said, "I haven't seen you for the past two days, and I've been meaning to talk to you . . . what happened the other night?"

Melinda asked, "What do you mean?"

Her roommate replied, "Well, I thought I heard a prowler in the house. Did you think you heard a prowler and maybe you went down to check it?"

"No," Melinda said.

"Well . . . I thought I heard things in the house. I thought I heard you, but you were in your room. So I went downstairs to see if there was anything to it. Maybe I was just being paranoid, but I thought I had better go look. So I went downstairs . . . and I came back up. And the light was on in your room, but your door was closed. So I looked in your room and you weren't there . . . so I figured maybe you were in the bathroom and then when I came back up, you had gone back in your room."

By now, Melinda was beginning to realize what had happened. She had never left her room, not consciously at least. And here was her roommate saying that her bedroom was empty. So not only did Melinda remember having missing time, but her roommate corroborated that Melinda was not even in her bedroom!

That wasn't all. Melinda's roommate dropped the bombshell. Melinda clearly recalled her words. "She said, 'I went back to bed and I thought I was just being ridiculous . . . I decided not to worry about it. I figured you must have gone back into your room. So I sat in bed reading. I read to try and fall asleep. Out of the corner of my eye . . . I saw a flash of light in the hallway. I glanced, thinking maybe you had opened up your door. . . . and the flash of light was moving, and then it stopped. Melinda, I saw the weirdest thing . . . I saw this being standing in the doorway. It was real small . . . . it came up to the handle on the door, and it had this great big over-sized head. Melinda, it was really scary . . . it had these eyes, these big dark eyes that wrapped around."

At that point, Melinda nearly passed out. Her roommate had just given a detailed description of a gray-type alien. However, the roommate was wondering if it was perhaps a ghost or something demonic. She later drew the figure and showed it to Melinda. Melinda was shocked. "This drawing is actually the most incredible and frightening picture of a gray. He has a large head, eyes wrapped around. She said it was tilting its head and looking at her as if to look out of the corner of his eye. So she drew it from that angle. She said, 'I saw this. After it stopped in my doorway and looked at me, it went through your closed door into your room. So I figured you must have known about it.'"

Melinda asked her roommate if she had ever seen anything like that before. Her roommate mentioned the book *Communion* by Whitley Strieber. The roommate then realized what she was saying. She said to Melinda, "Oh, my God! Did I see an alien?"

Melinda didn't know quite how to respond, and just filed the incident in the back of her mind. A few months later, her roommate's daughter moved in for a short stay. "The daughter also witnessed stuff happening to me," Melinda said. "In fact, it scared her so bad, the daughter moved out because of it. I was told the fourteen-year-old moved out to go back and live with her dad. Her parents were divorced. That's the story I was told. Actually she went back to live with her dad because she could not stay there any longer.

What she was experiencing was scaring her to death. This is what I ended up being told years later." By now, Melinda had considerable reason to believe she was having extraterrestrial contact, but she still had her doubts. "I was still really in denial about it, even with all that. I was just going, 'Oh, my goodness.'"

Meanwhile, she began to have other experiences. "I realize now this is somewhat of a pattern, that I feel upset or agitated before going to bed. Back then I didn't realize that meant something. Now I pay attention to stuff like that. But I went to bed feeling somewhat agitated, though I fell asleep quickly and slept very soundly. But I was woken up in the middle of the night by what sounded like something running around in my room. And I sat up in bed and it stopped. And I thought, 'Oh, it was just a bad dream.' I fell asleep and was woken up a little later by the same sound. But this time when I woke up, again it stopped. And I thought, 'This is ridiculous!' And I fell back asleep again. The third time I woke up, it continued. Even though I was sitting up in bed, I could still hear it. I turned on the light next to me and then it stopped. I was sitting in my bed completely awake before I turned on the light, shaking, reaching for the light. I was shaking so bad. And I heard this thing, and it sounded like something running around. I'm like, 'What the heck is it?' It scared me.

"And I turned on the light, and like I said, it stopped. Of course, at this point I'm thinking that maybe something is happening. And I tell you, the first time I woke up, it sounded like a very large thing walking around in my room. That's how I remember it, something large in my room . . . but the third time, it didn't sound like something large. It sounded like something small. . . .

"So then I sat there and it started up again. Well, then I realized that my curtains were moving. . . . It was a cold night, the window was closed. And I see my curtains move. I mean, my heart is going *b-b-b-b-b-b-b!* And I move my curtain and out flying from behind it is a dove, like a gray mourning dove. Now, there was a large windowsill outside these windows . . . and doves would gather on that . . . and in the morning some-times, I would be woken up to the sound of doves that were outside my window. That was not that unusual. But here, my window's closed, right? I have a screen that's nailed on. And my bedroom door is closed . . . when I went to bed that night, I closed my door and there was nothing in my room."

Melinda was left with a puzzling enigma. Not only had she heard something walking around, but now a bird had mysteriously appeared inside her bedroom. It was a physical impossibility, and yet there the bird was. "Of course I immediately checked to see if the window was open," Melinda recalled. "And not only was the window closed, but I had to open it to check the screen. And I'm thinking, 'You idiot, why are you even opening it? Obviously it was closed to begin with.' But I opened it and checked the screen. The screen was still nailed on."

Melinda's attention was drawn again to the dove, which was now thoroughly panicked and was bouncing off the mirrored sliding glass doors on Melinda's closet. Melinda threw a sweatshirt over the bird, gently bundled it up and carried it outside. "How did this thing manifest in my room? And here I had gone to bed feeling agitated . . . I don't know absolutely that something happened that night. But given the before going to bed thing, given the fact of how the bird materialized—I'm led to believe that something probably happened that night. Now the truth is I don't know. How the bird materialized in there, I don't know. But I'm thinking that the doves gathered on that sill sometimes in the morning, that if I had been taken and brought back, and they did take me through the window in that particular apartment. (I was familiar with that happening. I have memories of that happening.) But I was thinking that when they brought me back, that one of those poor doves sitting there next to the window got sucked in through the opening or whatever makes them able to do that . . . to me it was physical evidence that I had had something happen."

Melinda continued to have bizarre experiences, and she began to consider the idea of going to a hypnotist or hypnotherapist. "So all these things combined," she said. "Here I had the missing time, I had a roommate witnessing, I had woken up with matching bruises on my ankles and puncture marks on my knee. It was all this stuff . . . I was having all sorts of things start to surface . . . this I could tell was beyond my ability."

So when the opportunity for a hypnotic regression was offered to her, Melinda decided to accept. The regression was done by a well-known and highly respected UFO researcher and author. The regression itself was quite revealing. "I said stuff that I know is common in people's experiences but at the time I had never heard of it. Like the aliens bringing out a black box and showing it to me. I mean, that was a weird thing. I don't know . . . so what had come up was this experience of being shown a black box. I sat in a chair, and I remember the chair very clearly . . . it was like an 'Erector set' chair. It was metal—it was like brushed aluminum with holes cut out of it, so it looked like lattice-work . . . and it had really weird arms. It somewhat reclined and it was up kind of high. And I had to sit in this thing while they—it was almost like they did a play or skits in front of me. And they'd watch my reaction to violence, my reaction to murder, this thing with the black box. They gave me a gun, wanted me to shoot one of them, and I wouldn't. This is the kind of stuff that came up . . . would I shoot one of them? Would I kill one? What did I think if one killed the other? And then, like I said, this black box thing."

In the middle of her remembering this bizarre experience, Melinda suddenly recalled another experience when she was only fifteen. "Suddenly, I was back being fifteen, and had an experience where they were taking eggs from me, and I'm lying on a table. This was my first memory of something like this . . . I'm lying on a table. They have this long needle, they're inserting it in what I thought was my belly button . . . In the regression, I was very upset. I was crying. He [the hypnotherapist] was trying to calm me down. I had pain with it, not bad. And it was very frightening and very upsetting . . . I didn't know what they were removing. I said, 'They are removing tissue. I see stuff going up into a tube. There's blood . . .' I had no idea what they were taking from me. It was like, I have a needle in my stomach and they're sucking stuff out of me. I have no idea what. And it was going up into a tube, I could see that. It hurt. And it was really upsetting. So then he ended the regression."

Melinda and the researcher then discussed the results. He wanted to know if Melinda had heard of any of the details she was recounting, and she wanted to know if he had heard of any of it—if all of it was real.

Melinda assured him that it was all new to her. The researcher reassured Melinda as best as he could without actually "leading" her. When Melinda pressed him for a definite answer, the researcher said that only she could decide if her memories real. "Now I understand why he was reacting that way," she said. "Because he couldn't tell me. He didn't know if it was really happening, other than it matched stuff he knew. He couldn't say that. He was doing the right thing, and doing the right thing as a good researcher to not lead me in any way. . . ." Melinda continued to have a number of dramatic UFO experiences. She soon found another trustworthy UFO researcher/hypnotherapist and underwent several regressions. In each regression, she recalled more details that led her to realize she was in fact an abductee.

Then, in July 1991, less than three years following her introduction to the subject, Melinda and two friends had an experience in which all three were driving along a remote highway when they encountered a UFO. It was to be the single experience that proved to Melinda once and for all that extraterrestrials were a part of her life.

Melinda said, "I had become very good friends with these guys, and met both of them out on that trip to Area 51. That's where I originally met James and Robert (they requested that their real names not be used), and now they're, like, two of my best friends."

The three had heard of sightings occurring in Lancaster, California, a mere few hours away. They decided to do a little investigation and skywatch. They headed along the Angeles Crest Highway, which cuts across the mountains and considerably shortened their trip to Lancaster. The only drawback is that the roads are curvy and dark, and the road is somewhat remote. But as it was already 11:30 P.M., they decided to take the mountain route and save as much time as they could.

Melinda recalled, "So we're going over Angeles Crest to cut across the mountains. We started to drive and we're talking. And they brought this big high-powered light . . . a super-high-powered light that shoots this beam a quarter-mile. And they brought that for signaling them in. And we had walkie-talkies, and we had a scanner . . . and they set it to scan a couple of frequencies that were within what we thought were maybe the Edwards [Air Force Base] frequencies. They had their video camera and binoculars and all those kinds of things.

"So we took off and we're driving over Angeles Crest. And we had a couple of weird things happen that didn't really mean anything to us at the time. We kept seeing dogs. It was really late at night, we thought we were seeing wild dogs come out on the road. There was this discussion over animals. I think we saw an owl. Then there's this thing where we saw a deer. And it was like, "God! We saw an owl! We saw a deer! We're seeing so much wildlife."

"So then, we're driving along, eventually coming out from behind a bush, we see a coyote that kind of stops for a second and looks right at our car and ducks back. And we're like, 'Wow!' So all this kind of stuff was happening and we were arguing somewhat about it.

"We're driving along and Robert jokes, 'Let's call one down or whatever.' We're way up in the mountain now. But he has this light beam, he's leaning out the car window, and he's shooting the light up into space, and shooting it at the hills and doing stuff with it. And meanwhile, the scanner's on, and I think we're barely picking up anything. But he's shooting the light up for a while and playing with it. Eventually he stops and says, 'Gee, I wonder if we called any in?'

"And we're looking out the windows, looking to see if we had a sighting. And at one point, Robert says he sees something on the right. James and I are certain that we see something on the left. So then we start having this argument whether we're having a sighting on the right side of the car or the left side of the car. We were probably seeing two, but that didn't dawn on us until later. But we were seeing this . . . and we're driving along . . . just talking and stuff.

"The next thing we know, is that the scanner starts to malfunction and is making weird noises. They unhook the scanner and turn it off and on; it's still doing it. They're trying to fix the scanner, which is being really weird. And then the light wouldn't work. We tried to turn the light back on and it doesn't work. And it's weird that we're arguing now about why the scanner won't work and why the light won't work.

"We're driving along and eventually they get the scanner fixed, and eventually the light works again.

We got them both fixed. And then we all have to go to the bathroom really bad . . . they pull over and both guys are like, 'We can't wait.' They pull over and they jump out and they go . . . next to the vehicle."

Melinda elected to wait. The three exited the Angeles Crest Highway and drove the few remaining miles into Lancaster. They all agreed to stop at the nearest store because they had an incredible thirst. Melinda recalled, "We're like, 'God, we're thirsty!' I had to go to the bathroom. One of them had to go to the bathroom again."

Each of them bought large drinks and guzzled them down quickly. "I got a great big thing of [water]," Melinda said. "I drank the whole thing. That is so unlike me . . . one of them got a big bottle of water, drank it, and the other got a Big Gulp. We all drank our stuff. We're like, 'God, we're thirsty.'"

Then they noticed another strange detail. There was almost no traffic on what should have been a crowded freeway. As Melinda recalled, "We got to the freeway, we said, 'Boy, this place is dead.' We're thinking, it should be like midnight. There are no cars anywhere. We're thinking, maybe it could be 12:30, right? So James, he says, 'I wonder what time it is? It feels late. Doesn't it feel late? I'm kind of tired.' He pulls it [a watch] out. It's like 3:00 in the morning. We're going, 'What?!'. . . we were missing at the very least an hour and half of time.

"The drive out there is a little over two hours. But when you go over Angeles Crest, you can make it out there in about an hour and a half. This took us three and a half hours. There was no way . . . I mean, it was like a full two hours longer than it ever could have taken. We're like, 'That took us four hours. That's not possible!'"

They drove around Lancaster for a little while, trying to find the place they were looking for, with little luck. They finally set up a skywatch. However, shortly after they set up, they decided to pack up and go home.

As Melinda said, "James was in a bad mood. He's like, 'That's it, we're going.' We left. Robert fell asleep in the car. That was so weird for him to fall asleep in the car because he doesn't do that . . . he basically slept the whole way. He said, 'I have never slept in the car.' He said it was like he was drugged or something. It was weird. And James was in a really bad mood. I didn't say anything . . . it was the weirdest thing. Not like us. Here we realize, we knew that something had to have happened, but it was like we weren't going to talk about it. It was like the guys just couldn't deal with it. I said, 'Guys, let me tell you something, we've had two hours of missing time.' It was just like understood, we're not going to talk about it. They were very uncomfortable."

They continued the ride in silence and returned to their separate homes. Melinda continued to think about what had happened, and in the days that followed, began having powerful flashbacks of their evening. "It took me about two weeks to remember what happened. The next day, and within a number of days, I had inklings of when the car came to a stop on the road. And all of a sudden, it just started flooding forward. I remembered a whole bunch of stuff."

Melinda was stunned by her vivid memories. She had no way of knowing that 20 percent of abductees consciously remember their encounters in full detail. In a period of two weeks, she was able to account for all of the time she was aboard the craft. She decided to call James and ask him if he had any memories of what had happened.

He replied, "Well, maybe, yeah. I remember, but not a lot."

Melinda called Robert and asked him, "Do you remember?"

"No," he replied. "I haven't remembered anything. I've tried, and I've tried, and I don't remember anything."

Melinda met with James later to compare notes on what they had seen. It was to be a profound meeting that would stun them both into disbelief. Melinda said, "James, I really remember. I need to know if you remember."

James said, "Well, kind of."

Melinda said, "Well, what do you remember, tell me."

"Well, I don't know," James said. "I might be making it up."

"Just go with it," she prodded him. "Tell me."

James began to reveal a remarkable story that matched Melinda's recall to the degree that it was obvious that something real had happened. "I had not told him anything about my experience," Melinda remembered. "The only thing we had discussed is how the car had come to a stop. That one thing we did discuss, on the phone and when we got together prior to that. We discussed having the car come to a stop, and then we remembered an alien standing on the street in front of the car. It's looking at us, like mentally telling James to stop. And James just came to a stop. And I had asked him, 'Did you stop because you didn't want to hit him?'

"And he's like, 'No, it was just like I knew to stop the car.' And he was kind of standing over to the side. James kind of pulled over to the side and stopped. He was standing right in front of us. James said it was like he was under control to do it. He said, 'I don't know why I did it, I just did.' And we had remembered this being standing in front of the car, pretty much a typical gray. Definitely a gray, a five-foot gray. And it was definitely doing a 'mental whammy' on James, making him bring the car to a stop. James said it was almost like the car was under some kind of control, like the car just stopped. James said, 'It was like the car just stopped. I looked at this guy, the next thing I know, the car just comes to a stop.'

"I said, 'Well, did you do it?'

"He said, 'Well, I don't really remember doing it. Either I just did, or it did on its own.' And that's what we discussed.'

As they met on this particular evening, they were stunned to find that their memories matched event for event. "It matched," Melinda said. "I was saying, 'Yes, yes! Oh, my God! Yes! Oh, my God!' . . . it was verbatim to what I had remembered."

Eventually all three underwent hypnotic regression. For James and Melinda, the regression uncovered few new details, but served to verify what they had already consciously remembered. "James and I basically remembered the whole thing from beginning to end."

Robert, on the other hand, was only able to recall the beginning, a brief moment in the middle, and then part of the end. Why Robert was not able to fully recall the event may seem mysterious, but both Melinda and James remembered what happened and why Robert was not able to remember.

Their account remains one of the most incredible multiple-witness abductions on record. As Melinda recalled, "What had happened first before the car came to a stop, before we saw the aliens, Robert was playing with the light. We're having this argument about seeing a UFO. After, he saw something to the right. James and I saw something to the left of the car, just lights, moving lights in the sky. And the next thing is, there's a series of bright flashes, three bright flashes in the car. Robert wigs. He says, 'Ahh! What is that?!' Robert says, 'What the hell!' And I was like, 'Whoa!' . . . so then the flash of light stops, the car comes to a stop, there's an alien there, suddenly, and some other aliens come out either down the road or off the ship. They were suddenly there . . . What we remembered happening is, the alien in front of the car is still standing there, but other ones come who are standing next to the car . . . they come around to the side of the car and open up James' door. James gets out of the car fully on his own, and starts walking . . . there's a big mountain on the side of the road, and the mountain goes up on the right, and a there's this cliff to the left, a sheer drop off the side of the mountain . . . and there's a ship . . . even with the road is a UFO that doesn't seem to be on anything; it seems to be hovering or stationary in the air. And there's a ramp. This is so cliché, but this is what we independently remembered, that there's a ramp or a walkway of some kind coming down from the UFO to the road, even though the UFO was just hovering out directly off the cliff from the side of the road . . . It looked like it was large and multilayered. It had stuff on it. It wasn't smooth. It was like a wedding cake, multitiered . . . he [James] and I both remember it being large, being multilayered with something on top. And that the ramp seemed to be black or dark.

"Anyway, two beings come over. They open up James' door, and he gets out, or he opens up his door and gets out, and they're basically staying next to him . . . they come to Robert's door, they open up Robert's door. Robert goes, 'Ahh!' This all happened pretty quick. Robert seemed to be reacting out of fright. They touch him on his temples . . . and his head goes down. His head sinks and he's put out. Meanwhile, I see them start to get Robert out of the car. Robert gets out of the car on his own, but isn't like completely on his own. His head is down, his shoulders are down. I was really concerned because he's moving, but not necessarily of his own free will. He seemed half out of it. He seemed like he was drugged. And I was concerned."

At this point, the aliens had secured both James and Robert and were leading them toward the craft hovering over the cliffside. Melinda was left alone in the car wondering what would happen next. "I'm sitting there, and the guys are getting out of the car. Next thing I know, I'm floating up . . . I just remember floating out. Because I thought, 'Nobody's at my door.' And that concerned me. I thought I was going to be left there. And I'm thinking, 'Don't hurt my friends. Don't take my friends! Don't take my friends! Oh, my God! These guys aren't going to be able to deal with this! Oh, my God! They've never had this happen.' I started to have these thoughts. I thought they were going to leave me there. I was in a blind panic. Because they came to their door and they got out, and I'm still sitting in the back seat. They're completely out of the car and I'm thinking, 'They're going to leave me here.' And the next thing I know, I start to raise out of the seat, and then I'm going back, and I was like, 'Whoa!' I think I even touched the roof, and I floated out the back. And they recalled my being floated out the back. James turned to see me floating upside down in the back of his Jeep . . . he said, 'I thought you were really scared because you wouldn't get out. The next thing I know, you're floating out the back.'

"The next thing I know," Melinda continued, "is I am standing there. As soon as I had gotten out the back, my legs were on the ground. I'm standing behind the Isuzu Trooper with the back door open. I had one alien on either side of me. I saw James walking with two behind him. He's walking ahead of them, walking up the ramp into the ship. And I'm thinking, 'Oh, my God! James is under alien influence because he would never just do that on his own. Oh, my God! What have they done to my friend?'

"Robert, I see him standing out in front of the car with two aliens on either side of him with his head slumped down, and . . . I was really concerned . . . James was showing no fear at all. He was showing no fear, and I was really freaked by that. And here's Robert who was out of it with his head down. And to get him to walk, they were poking him in the back. He would take a couple of steps and stop. And then they would come up and push him again. And then he'd take a couple of more steps and he'd stop. And they were like just push—walk, walk, walk, stop . . . push—walk, walk, walk, stop . . . push. They were pushing him along to get him to keep walking because he was out of it.

"I was so scared for them. When they started to walk up the ramp, I then followed behind them. And I had aliens on either side of me, but they were just walking with me . . . I didn't want to go, but I was so concerned for my friends. I felt like I had to watch out for them. So I walked up after them. I thought, 'These guys aren't going to be able to handle this. These guys are going to be destroyed by this. . . . They've never had this happen to them.' And I was literally telling them, 'Don't hurt my friends.'

"So we walked up onboard, and we were in a small room. It's fairly dimly lit, but we're standing in a lit-up area. And the floor is black. I remember it being like black rubber, like hard rubber. We were standing there and they proceeded to undress us in front of each other. And I'm thinking . . . these guys, being forced to undress in front of each other and in front of me, for them to have to stand naked in front of me—oh, my

God, I feel so bad for them.' . . . I was so worried about how they were going to react. And they, in later regressions, were also worried. Robert does remember being undressed a little. He did remember that a little, but he was concerned about me. He remembers being concerned for me. And James was really concerned, thinking, 'Oh, Melinda's going to be so embarrassed. I feel so bad for her. This is no big deal to me.' That's what he was thinking.

"Well, I was thinking the same exact thing, which was, 'I'm okay with this. It's no big deal.' And I was trying to look at them with reassurance, nodding . . . so they undressed the three of us. We're standing there, staring at each other without anything on. But it wasn't a big deal to any of us. And then they walked us out of this room into a brightly lit room. And there were two tables and this large chair-thing. It reminds me not too much like a dentist's chair, but more like a big old-fashioned barber's chair, but high-tech, large and well padded with a big headrest, and big armrest.

"They sit Robert in that chair. They instruct James to get up on one table and me to get up on the other. And the tables are in a T-position but with space in-between them. Robert is . . . in this big chair, and they put this like headphone unit, this headpiece on Robert. He's still out of it and he's looking straight ahead. His eyes were glazed, straight ahead, like the lights were on but nobody's home.

"The first thing they do is, I'm lying on a table, and they're examining me. But with James—my first memory was that James was screaming. I thought he was in pain and they were hurting him. James remembered this, and he said, 'They grabbed for me down there. And they were like feeling me . . . I was like, what the hell?' . . . and screamed at them in total surprise.

"I said, 'Oh, my, God . . . I saw you scream, but I thought when they grabbed you, you were in agony when you screamed.'"

As it turned out, James was in no pain at all. He was merely startled and somewhat angered. The aliens proceeded to examine him, and expressed particular interest in an old surgical scar. Meanwhile, Melinda had no idea what was happening. "I was watching this. Now in retrospect, I realize that they were wanting me to watch this. And I'm still sitting there, watching what they're doing.

"Meanwhile, Robert's still sitting in the chair, totally out of it. He's got headphones on and is just glazed over. And I'm thinking . . . they're torturing James. He's in pain. They're going to do something to us. They're hurting him.' They looked like they were going to do surgery down there. And I'm thinking, 'Oh, my God! What are they doing to do to James?' I remember thinking, 'I hope they're only taking sperm.'

"Meanwhile, I'm really concerned for Robert. I'm thinking . . . they're brainwashing Robert. What are they doing to Robert? What are they going to make him do?' This is what I was thinking, because he had this headset on and he was so out of it. I'm thinking, 'What kind of mind control are they going to do on him? Are they telling him to do something? Are they programming him? Are they deprogramming him? What the hell is that?' I was really disturbed by that.

"I even said, 'What are you doing to him?'

"They said they were giving him information. I said, 'What are you giving him?'

"And they said, 'It's all right, we're giving him information.'

"'What is it?'

"'It's all right. We're educating him.'

"This was all telepathy. 'What are you doing to my friend? Don't hurt my friend.'

"And they said, 'We're not hurting him. He's all right. It's all right.' They don't give you straight answers. They say, 'It's okay. We need to do this. You understand.'

"So meanwhile, I'm escorted off my table, back behind where the table is, into another room through a curved doorway. It is about forty or fifty feet in diameter. But the aliens make a circle around me. They put me in the middle of the room, and put a circle around me. And there's quite a few of them. There are like twelve or fifteen huddled around me. And the tall female one that has kind of been my handler, and another kind of tall one, they said, 'Now, we're going to do something, and don't be afraid. But this is very important that we do this. We're going to put this over your head.'

"So they had this thing that looked like a bag, a mesh-bag with black fabric. I remembered it almost being like metal, a metal fabric. It was loosely woven, it wasn't like tight fabric. It was loose. They took this bag and put it over my head and over my shoulders, and then they tighten the bottom of it. It goes way up on my shoulders almost to where my elbows are. And when they tighten it in, it holds my arms in. I can move my hands from the elbows down, but my elbows are held in by this tight thing. And it's around my head. I panic at first because I don't think I'm going to be able to breathe. And I can't see. It wasn't pitch black. I could see a little bit of light. It wasn't tightly woven because I could see light through the holes. I could tell that the lights were on in the room. And at first I panicked because I didn't think I was going to be able to breathe. I was like, [heavy respirations] 'Oh, my God! I can't see and I can't breathe and I can't move my arms.' And the next thing I knew, I couldn't move my legs either. And actually my arms were down at my side too, so I could not move my arms or my legs. I was standing perfectly straight. They had me stand with my feet together. They instructed me to put my feet together. So I had my feet together, my arms at my side, the bag-thing on my head, and I could not move.

"The next thing I know, I feel one of them push me. And I wanted to move my foot to—you know, I was starting to fall over. But I couldn't move my foot to brace myself from falling. It was very frightening. And another one catches me on the other side and pushes me. Then another one pushed me. They'd push me and I'd fall way over and then another would catch me. And I could feel myself being caught and tossed back. And I felt like—when you're a kid, you play with one of those punching clowns? I thought, 'I'm a punching clown!' I mean, that's exactly what came to my mind while this was going on.

"But it was really scary because I thought I was going to fall. I have a fear of falling. And each time, I didn't know if someone was going to catch me. I thought, 'If I hit the ground, I'm dead weight. From full standing with the force of being pushed, I'm going to go bam!' And they kept doing this. And at first, I was getting pretty low before they would catch me. And then after a while, it wasn't so bad. It was more like just rocking back and forth. And after awhile, I realized, 'I don't think they're going to drop me.' I caught on. I mean, at first it was very scary. I was terrified. Then I realized, 'They're not going to drop me.' And I just relaxed and gave into it. I thought, 'Okay, this is some kind of exercise.' And then when I really relaxed and just gave into it, then it almost started being—I don't know if 'fun' is the word, but it was kind of like it was amusing in that this was a trip that they were doing this.' I was kind of laughing at the fact that this was a really weird thing for them to do. This was really weird.

"When I finally got to that state of mind, they stopped. And I was stood back up. And they took the bag off, lifted it off. Then they instructed me to walk. All of a sudden, I was able to move again. And they were saying, 'You needed to learn that.'

"I didn't know what the lesson was. Now I realize they were helping me to get over my fear of falling. When they stopped is when I finally trusted them. It was also a lesson in trusting them . . . when I was okay with it, that's when they stopped. And they said, 'You needed to learn to trust us.'

"And I was pissed at them. Then they took me out of that room and they put me back on the table. They had James, they were basically done with James, and I didn't know what they had done with him in there, but they had him sitting and facing me. And they proceeded to do a gynecological thing with me, where they took a bunch of eggs from me. And they had James watch. I was really upset. I thought, 'This is really going to freak James out.'

"And it turned out later in his memory of it, he was upset thinking, 'This is going to freak Melinda out.' . . .

in our separate memories, both of us were feeling concerned about the other person."

The aliens continued to perform a gynecological procedure. Robert was still sitting, unconscious, in the large chair wearing a helmet-like device. Melinda continued her story. "Eventually they stopped and they cleaned me up, and they cleaned James up, and they got us off the table. They removed the headpiece. They get Robert off the chair; Robert, at this point, stands. He was gaining consciousness, because he stood up out of the chair on his own. And he was looking around, like, 'Hey, how are you guys doing? Hey, how did we get here?' He looked kind of scared, like he was looking at me and he couldn't talk, but he wanted to say, 'Are you okay?' And I think later he said that he consciously said that he was looking at us, saying, 'Are you guys okay? What happened to you?' So again, it was like he was concerned about us. And he was also like, 'What just happened to me? I don't remember anything.' That's what he remembered that he was thinking. His thoughts were, 'Are they as aware of what's going on as I am?'

"And then they took us back into the small room, the first one, and they got us dressed again. I don't really remember how they did that. I know that we somewhat helped, especially getting dressed again, because we were like, 'Oh, good. It's over.' We were somewhat dressing ourselves. When they undressed us, it happened very fast. But when we left, we were kind of dressing ourselves. And they walked us back.

"They put Robert back in the car. I opened the door on the side and got in the normal way. James got back in, they closed James' door. They backed off. The car was turned back on. The ship takes off, and we're driving down the road, commenting about the fact that the scanner is malfunctioning.

"When they stopped the car, Robert was leaning out the window with the light in his hand. And he set it down after they stopped the car. When the car was turned back on . . . they gave him the light to hold and they put him back with the light. So the next thing is, he's still got the light in his hand, but now it won't work. And the scanner's malfunctioning. And we're talking about the fact that the light isn't working properly, and the scanner's malfunctioning."

They drove on down the road and shortly discovered that they had experienced missing time. The rest is history. The account is, in most respects, a standard alien abduction case. However, each case does have its unique elements, and this case is no exception.

First, as a multiple-witness abduction account with corroborated testimony, it is rarer than most cases. The examinations described by Melinda are, of course, commonly reported. Less common was what happened to Melinda when she left the room onboard the UFO.

They tossed her back and forth in a bizarre game that seems in some ways, absurd. However, as it turns out, this exact process is used in acting classes to develop trust among fellow actors. Many other cases on record also contain bizarre exercises in trust. Months later, Melinda had another similar experience that was even more terrifying. One evening, as she lay in bed, she experienced herself being levitated up toward a UFO. Just when she was about to enter, she was dropped. She fell in total terror about fifty feet down, thinking that she was falling to her death. Just at the point where she would have hit, she was suddenly levitated back up towards the UFO, only to be dropped again! This went on several times and Melinda began to wonder if they were playing some cruel game of cat and mouse. After awhile, however, again Melinda realized that they weren't going to let her be harmed, and she let go of her fear. Not surprisingly, they stopped the game. It turned out to be apparently another somewhat brutal yet effective game of trust.

Melinda was also curious about what James remembered happening to him while she was in the other room. The story was more incredible than she first thought. "James said when I was out of the room, they came over to him, and they showed him a device, a bunch of stuff. And they told him how to make a UFO detector, and they gave him the information. And he said they said because they wanted him to document and videotape them. When sightings happen, they told him he has a mission to document this stuff . . . so they showed him how to do it. This is how it works. You have a magnetic current with two magnets, and whenever there's a strong enough field, it'll break that. It was really super simple . . . it was really a weak magnetic field between two magnets set at a distance. And that's what they showed him. And I was like, 'Yeah, right.' But he said, 'No, when you were gone, they showed me this. They showed me how to do this. And they explained the whole thing technically to me, and I was given the information how to build those.' He said, 'They were done and they made sure I understood, and I said, yes, I understand.' He said, 'When I understood, that's when they brought you back. Once I understood, I just sat there and they were telling me some other stuff.' And he doesn't really remember everything they were telling him, but they were telling him other stuff, and then they brought me back into the room."

Another mystery that was partially revealed was why Robert was unable to recall most of the experience; he was unconscious most of the time. "We got regressed separately," Melinda recalled. "And our regression stories matched. And when Robert started to get details, the details he got did match, even though he was not able to get a lot of it. In regression, Robert gets to a certain point where he has a violent sensation. The chair starts to spin and he literally feels he's doing flips in the chair . . . he can remember up to where they came up to the car door, and the car door opens, and the next thing he knows, he feels this violent sensation. So it fits with what we remember happened to him, which is they touched him on the forehead and shut him off."

There was yet another bizarre detail that has turned up in other abduction accounts, but is rare. James consciously recalled seeing a human-looking male aboard the UFO dressed in what appeared to be a blue military uniform, standing in the background, watching the whole abduction take place. Melinda also recalled seeing the military man during a regression, and afterwards, she found out that James had seen the same thing and remembered it consciously.

As Melinda remembered, "James said that during the whole thing, as soon as we were taken onboard until we were taken off, there was a guy in dressed blue standing over the side, not in full dress, but a long-sleeved blue shirt and slacks, dark blue, a Navy uniform. James asked, 'Don't you remember?' I said, 'No,' He said, 'Yeah, he was standing over there in parade rest, like he was monitoring and watching the whole thing.'"

At that point, Melinda remembered that she had in fact recalled the military man during her regression. She called up the UFO researcher who performed the regression and asked her to check her file. The researcher confirmed, "You said that under regression . . . all three of you guys independently remembered seeing this guy in military uniform standing in the background watching."

Afterwards, all three went through various reactions to the experience. There were expected periods of denial and disbelief. A lot of different theories were raised. The presence of someone from the military concerned them and they wondered about mind-control experiments. To this day, they remain unsure what happened. They only know something happened. For Melinda, however, hearing James afterwards describe to her what happened, without ever having heard her tell any details, and having it match perfectly with her own perception, it was validation to a degree that left her convinced of the reality of the experience.

To this day, Melinda has had literally dozens of UFO experiences. On one occasion, she was taken onboard and was shown holographic films of upcoming natural disasters. On another occasion, she was shown a hybrid alien and was told that it was her own child. During some of her other experiences, there have been other military personnel present.

Melinda's experiences may sound unusual, but again, they fit the pattern. Like most abductees, she has confirmation by multiple witnesses supporting her account. Today Melinda maintains an interest in UFOs, and has been looking into other cases like her own that also involve a military presence.

Conclusion

For each case included in this book, there are many others that were excluded, usually because the witnesses were not available for an interview. For example, there was a case involving a young couple who had an encounter while camping in the desert. They awoke and climbed out of their tent to find several small gray-type aliens floating on a cliffside directly above them, picking small plants, and putting them into tiny plastic containers. At that point, they suddenly lost consciousness, waking up later inside their tent.

Another case involved a truck driver who, on his route, encountered several small humanoid figures standing by the side of the road. At the same moment that he realized the figures looked very unusual, he heard a voice in his head telling him not to be afraid. At this point, he experienced a period of missing time. Afterward, he was completely and understandably traumatized.

Another uninvestigated case involved a young woman who was sleeping with her husband when she was awakened by a light coming in her bedroom window. She looked to see a gray-type alien glowing in blue light hovering and looking at her. She tried to awaken her husband, but he couldn't be roused. Moments later, she unaccountably fell asleep. A few days later, they had visitors at the house asking about the previous tenant, an older woman who had recently moved. When told that she was no longer living there, the visitors expressed disappointment and told the startled current residents that the former tenant used to call down UFOs, and had done so successfully for them on several occasions. Many other such cases exist, but they all follow the same pattern.

But are people really having these encounters? Is it possible that there is a mundane explanation? Skepticism of these types of stories still remains strong in society. Many people simply do not believe that people are actually having these experiences.

How the UFO skeptic survives could be a book in itself. Generally, the skeptic feels that these stories can be explained as lies or misperceptions. Often they are unaware of the vast amount of evidence in support of these encounters, or of the high credibility of many of the witnesses. On the other hand, an overly zealous UFO advocate can hinder research progress in the phenomenon as much as a skeptic. The ideal is to remain objective and study these accounts without any prejudiced agenda. Let us try to explain the accounts in this book using the theories raised by both skeptics and believers.

First, let's consider the possibility that the accounts may be the result of hoaxes or lies. Perhaps none of the people in this book are telling the truth and are telling outright lies. Of course, this possibility exists, but how likely is it? Certainly there is motive. Perhaps these people are lying simply to get attention. Being labeled a UFO contactee would definitely make a witness feel "special." Though one might point out that several of the witnesses have shunned all publicity and, especially for this book, have insisted upon anonymity. This would seem to lend credence to their stories. But then again, the psychology of lying is very complex. Not everyone tells an incredible story just to get attention. Some lie just for the satisfaction of having fooled the investigator. Some lie for perhaps pathological reasons. If these people are lying for attention, most are in for a rude awakening. People are just as likely to disbelieve or ridicule a witness as they are to bestow belief or praise.

One might also point out that many of the witnesses have a high level of credibility. These cases involve witnesses that include a medical doctor, an airplane mechanic, a housewife, a military man, a therapist, a waitress, an actor, a factory worker, a store manager, and an office worker. These are all people who have held jobs and are functional socially. Still, this doesn't mean they are not lying. After all, presidents, police officers, and high church officials have all been caught in lies. Position in society is not a perfect indicator of truth.

However the witnesses do not stand alone. In Jay Broman's case, there were, in fact, hundreds of witnesses. Laura Caigoy's case also involved her son. Rob Baldwin's case involved four people, all of whom experienced missing time. Dr. Nelson's case involved another witness who also experienced missing time. Rose and William Shelhart were also abducted together. Pat Brown and Marianne both had witnesses to their UFO sightings. Jack Stevens was abducted in front of his mother and brother, both of whom remember parts of the experience. Melinda Leslie was abducted with two friends, and also had two other witnesses who saw aliens in the house when she was being visited.

With so many supporting witnesses, the possibility that these experiences can be explained as lies is greatly diminished. Furthermore, the majority of the cases were referred to me by other people who vouched for the witnesses' credibility.

Probably the best argument that these people are lying is that their stories are, admittedly, fantastic. Inhuman creatures, silent hovering metallic disks, levitating beams of light, telepathic conversations, missing time—these are certainly not everyday events. Ironically, however, it is these same details that provide the strongest evidence these people are telling the truth. In other words, the corroborative details, the sheer consistency of the reports, virtually exclude any remaining possibility that the reports are the result of lies or hoaxes.

However, just because the hoax explanation fails to explain all the facts doesn't exclude the possibility that the reports may be the result of misperceptions. Maybe these people really believe they are having close encounters but are extremely fantasy-prone or gullible.

There is very little evidence to support this angle. The only reason this theory is even raised is because of the fantastic and bizarre elements of UFO encounter reports. This is akin to labeling a person as violent because he or she was a *victim* of a violent crime. A person is not defined by an experience as much as how the person *reacts* to the experience. As we have seen, the reactions to a UFO experience are as individual and unique as the people who have them.

Again, the encounter reports, although bizarre, are nevertheless consistent. The ten cases in this book represent a fair sample of these types of cases. Nine out of ten cases include the feature of missing time. Nine out of ten cases include the presence of alien beings. The reports of the beings are also remarkable consistent. In Jay Broman's case, there was missing time, but he had no memory of beings. In two of the other cases, the beings were not described other than being short. All the others involve some variation of the commonly reported gray humanoid—short, uniformed, large hairless heads, and large dark eyes. Yet none seemed to be described in exactly the same way. In other words, the differences seem to be pronounced enough to say that the witnesses are all dealing with different beings. Two of the cases involve beings that the witnesses described as more human than "gray-type" aliens. There is only one case involving the presence of military personnel during a UFO experience.

Fifty percent of the cases involve physiological reactions. One case involved unexplained nosebleeds. One involved a missing fetus. Another involved an interrupted menstrual cycle. Five involved unexplained scars, cuts, or bruises. One involved an apparent "healing." One involved two apparent "implants." There were other miscellaneous physiological reactions. One case also involved a "heat beam" from a UFO. One case involved a beam that caused static electricity and a coppery taste in the mouth. One case involved extreme thirst and an extreme need to urinate following an abduction. In two of the cases, witnesses were placed in a trance state. In one case, the witness fell asleep immediately following an abduction.

Seventy percent of the cases involve dialogues between the extraterrestrials and the abductees. In two of the cases, the conversation was one-sided and essentially limited to the aliens instructing the witnesses not to be afraid. One case involved a conversation revealing spiritual information. In another case, the aliens explained how they are helping humanity without getting too involved. In another case, the aliens explained how they siphoned electricity out of high-tension wires and attempted to impart mathematical knowledge. Another case involved considerable information concerning alien origins, as well as information about future events. Yet another case involved limited conversation about the procedures as they are being performed aboard the UFO, scientific information, and also reveals alleged prophecies of future events.

For those who described onboard encounters, the descriptions of the inside of the craft were also remarkably consistent. All reported the interior as "clean." All reported seeing technological instruments, usually computer-like, and strange lighting. Two cases involve the specific color of bronze. Four cases involve examinations on tables. Ninety percent of the cases involve UFO sightings, and 80 percent involve sightings of solid metallic-looking craft.

There were other types of physical evidence present. One case involved landing traces in the form of apparent "crop circles." In another case, the witness awoke with her bed full of twigs and her clothes dirty. In another case, the witness associated a lingering foul odor with her extraterrestrial contact. Then, of course, there was Jack Stevens' report of what appeared to be a foreign object first in his mouth, and then in his foot. One case involved a bird that mysteriously materialized in her bedroom. One case involves a motorcycle that was repaired during the encounter.

There are two cases which involve strange animals: one a large spotted skunk-like creature, and the other coyotes, deer, and owls.

Another form of evidence that appeared in the cases is electromagnetic effects. In one case, a UFO beam caused the car headlights to dim. In another case, the car was stalled by a UFO beam. In another, a car battery was dead following the encounter. Another case involved failure of a radio, a scanner, a flashlight, and a car engine.

The witnesses' psychological reactions to their experiences also followed some surprising patterns. Not surprisingly, many felt shock, disbelief, awe, and some fear. What was surprising, however, is that in 40 percent of the cases, the witnesses declined to talk about the event after it happened. One would think that after having a close encounter with a UFO, it would remain the topic of discussion for the next several days, if not weeks. But apparently, this is not the case.

Another interesting factor is that in 70 percent of the cases, witnesses remembered their encounter without the aid of hypnosis. Only 30 percent of the cases involved hypnosis. There are only two cases in which the witnesses used hypnosis to gain their first recall of what happened. In other words, hypnosis played only a minor role. The bulk of the information is from conscious recall.

The encounters have occurred all across the United States, including Arizona, California, Idaho, Michigan, New Mexico, New Jersey, and Washington. In 40 percent of the cases, the encounters occurred in a dense suburb area. In 60 percent of the cases, the encounters occurred while driving at night on a remote road.

Another interesting factor is that 100 percent of the cases involved not just one encounter, but multiple encounters. If not a series of sightings, the witnesses report a series of face-to-face encounters or more than one missing-time episode.

Interestingly, none of the witnesses reported their experiences as being entirely negative. Not one felt that the aliens are evil. Thirty percent of the cases involved people who were frightened by their ordeals.

In 60 percent of the cases, there was little or no trauma involved. In 40 percent of the cases, the witnesses feel that they have had decidedly positive experiences.

What other conclusions can be drawn from all of the above reports? Obviously, something is happening. But, *extraterrestrials?*

As incredible as this theory is, it is still the theory that best explains all the evidence. If UFOs aren't extraterrestrial objects, what then are they?

These ten accounts clearly describe solid craft that can perform amazing maneuvers, as well as beings that are amazingly consistent with reports from witnesses across the world. All the evidence points toward one fact: extraterrestrials are here.

■　■　■

Of course, UFOs are real. I am convinced that any rational person, who takes an objective look at the vast amount of evidence, will feel the same way. UFOs may be one of the most persistent and perplexing mysteries of the modern age, however, we are finally getting a picture of what is going on. The evidence comes in many forms including eyewitness testimony, lie detector tests, moving film, radar-visual cases, photographs, landing traces, medical effects, electromagnetic effects, medical evidence, animal evidence, metal fragments, and thousands of pages of declassified government documents from across the world.

The main purpose of this book is to present a small portion of new evidence, to add another piece of the puzzle toward solving the UFO mystery. The witnesses have been allowed to tell their encounters in their own words. There were no translations—all are true accounts told by real people about experiences that actually happened to them.

In most respects, I think the ten accounts corroborate what other researchers have found. There are silent hovering craft, gray-type aliens abducting people on levitating beams, telepathic communication, missing time, and the normal residue of effects both physical and psychological.

There were, of course, some surprises. The fact that most of the witnesses feel that the aliens are benign or even friendly—this was unexpected, especially considering the traumatic nature of their experiences. However, this attitude was also very consistent. Another surprise was that some of the cases involved nearly "human-like" aliens. With the superabundance of gray-type aliens, reports of human-like aliens are rare. Also rarely reported is the "Praying Mantis" figure in Dr. Nelson's case.

While abduction is the term usually used to describe these experiences, it is not necessarily accurate. Two of the cases involve voluntary onboard UFO experiences, in which the witnesses report that they were there on their own free will. When asked if they were given the choice to terminate all contact with extraterrestrials, all reported in the negative.

There were also several unique elements that, to my knowledge, have not been reported elsewhere in the UFO literature. An example is Sherry Jamison's report that the extraterrestrials repaired her motorcycle. Another is Jack Stevens' report of being dangled below the UFO to view the transfer of electricity from power lines to the craft. Marianne's account of aliens that live beneath the ocean is also highly unusual. Melinda Leslie's experience of being pushed back and forth by extraterrestrials is also unique. Other rare details reported by the witnesses include the presence of military personnel onboard a UFO, being taken to an area with rock-like walls, a robotic figure.

Another surprise was the highly spiritual nature of some of the cases. In a few of the cases, the witnesses appear to have been able to move beyond the typical abduction scenario and receive positive results from their experiences. The accounts of healings, spiritual information, helpful acts, long interactive conversations—60 percent of the cases were of this nature. These cases also involve people who have faced their experiences head-on or are comfortable with the fact that they are abductees.

Obviously the UFO phenomenon is extremely complex. But finally, a clearer picture emerges. The controversy now is not whether or not UFOs and aliens are visiting us. Rather, why are they here? What exactly are they doing? And how are we going to deal with it? UFO research today is grappling with questions like these. Are the aliens friendly? Should we try to contact them? Are they dangerous?

The only people who can honestly answer these questions are the people who've had close encounters. That is why I let the witnesses speak in their own words. They have all asked these questions for themselves, and if you read their accounts carefully, they have also answered them to various degrees.

The one question that's most difficult to answer is: what will happen next? There has been steady UFO activity for thousands of years and it certainly shows no signs of abating. Like it or not, UFOs are here to stay. If UFO activity continues to escalate as it has, sooner or later there will be conclusive proof of extraterrestrial visitation. A very real possibility exists that one day, extraterrestrials may eventually interact more openly and become a permanent presence among humanity. Hopefully, when that day comes, we will be prepared.

Suggested Reading

The following books all focus on close encounters with UFOs and contact with extraterrestrials.

Aronson, Virginia. *Celestial Healing. Close Encounters that Cure.* New York: Signet Books, 1999.

Bethurum, Truman. *Aboard a Flying Saucer.* Los Angeles, Calif.: DeVorss & Co., Publishers, 1954.

Bowen, Charles. *The Humanoids. A Survey of Worldwide Reports of Landings of Unconventional Aerial Objects and Their Occupants.* Chicago, Ill.: Henry Regnery Company, 1969.

Boylan, Richard J. *Close Extraterrestrial Encounters. Positive Experiences with Mysterious Visitors.* Tigard, Ore.: Wild Flower Press, 1994.

Bryan, C. D. B. *Close Encounters of the Fourth Kind. Alien Abduction, UFOs and the Conference at MIT.* New York: Alfred A. Knopf, 1995.

Buhler, Dr. Walter K.; Guilherme Pereira; Prof. Ney Matiel Pires. *UFO Abduction at Mirassol: A Biogenetic Experiment.* Tucson, Ariz.: UFO Photo Archives, 1985.

Bullard, Thomas E. *UFO Abductions. The Measure of a Mystery.* (The Fund for UFO Research) Glendale, Calif.: The Book Tree, 1987.

Cahill, Kelly. *Encounter.* New York: HarperCollins Publishers, 1996.

Cannon, Dolores. *The Custodians. Beyond Abduction.* Huntsville, Ark.: Ozark Mountain Publishing, 1999.

Carlsberg, Kim. *Beyond My Wildest Dreams. Diary of a UFO Abductee.* Santa Fe, N. Mex.: Bear & Company Publishing, 1995.

Casellato, Rodolfo R., Joao Valerio da Silva, and Wendelle C. Stevens. *UFO Abduction at Botucatu. A Preliminary Report.* Tucson, Ariz.: Wendelle C. Stevens, 1985.

Clear, Constance. *Reaching for Reality. Seven Incredible True Stories of Alien Abduction.* San Antonio, Tex.: Consciousness Now, Inc., 1999.

Collings, Beth & Anna Jamerson. *Connections. Solving Our Alien Abduction Mystery.* Newberg, Ore.: Wild Flower Press, 1996.

Dennett, Preston. *One In Forty: The UFO Epidemic. True Accounts of Close Encounters with UFOs.* Commack, N.Y.: Kroshka Books, 1996.

———. *UFO Healings: True Accounts of People Healed by Extraterrestrials.* Mill Springs, N.C.: Wild Flower Press, 1996.

———. *UFOs Over Topanga Canyon.* St. Paul, Minn.: Llewellyn Publications, 1999.

Druffel, Ann and D. Scott Rogo. *The Tujunga Canyon Contacts. Updated Edition.* New York: Signet Books, 1988.

Fiore, Edith. *Encounters: A Psychologist Reveals Case Studies of Abductions by Extraterrestrials.* New York: Doubleday, 1989.

Fowler, Raymond E. *The Allagash Abductions. Undeniable Evidence of Alien Intervention.* Tigard, Ore.: Wild Flower Press, 1993.

———. *The Andreasson Affair.* Englewood Cliffs, N.J.: Prentice Hall, Inc., 1979.

———. *The Andreasson Affair. Phase Two.* Englewood Cliffs, N.J.: Prentice Hall, Inc., 1982.

———. *The Watchers. The Secret Design Behind UFO Abduction.* New York: Bantam Books, 1990.

Gaevard, Prof. A. J. and Wendelle C. Stevens. *UFO Abduction at Maringa: The Agripa Experiment*. Tucson, Ariz.: Wendelle C. Stevens, 1987.

Haley, Leah A. *Lost Was the Key*. Tuscaloosa, Ala.: Greenleaf Publications, 1993.

Hickson, Charles and William Mendes. *UFO Contact at Pascagoula*. Tucson, Ariz.: Wendelle C. Stevens, 1983.

Hopkins, Budd. *Intruders. The Incredible Visitations at Copley Woods*. New York: Random House, 1987.

———. *Missing Time. A Documented Story of UFO Abductions*. New York: Richard Marek Publishers, 1981.

———. *Witnessed: the True Story of the Brooklyn Bridge UFO Abductions*. New York: Pocket Books, 1996.

Hough, Peter and Moyshe Kalman. *The Truth about Alien Abductions*. Wellington House, London: Blandford, 1997.

Imbrogno, Philip J. and Marianne Horrigan. *Contact of the 5th Kind*. St. Paul, Minn.: Llewellyn, 1997.

Jacobs, David. *Secret Life*. New York: Simon & Schuster, 1992.

———. *The Threat*. New York: Simon Schuster, 1998.

Johnson, Frank. *The Janos People. A Close Encounter of the Fourth Kind*. Sudbury, Suffolk: Neville Spearman Ltd., 1980.

Jordan, Debbie and Kathy Mitchell. *Abducted! The True Story of the Intruders Continues.* New York: Carroll & Graf Publishers, Inc., 1994.

Kent, Malcolm. *The Terror Above Us.* New York: Tower Books, 1967.

Kinder, Gary. *Light Years. An Investigation into the Extraterrestrial Experiences of Eduard Meier.* New York: Atlantic Monthly Press, 1987.

Lorenzen, Coral and Jim. *Abducted! Confrontations with Beings from Outer Space.* New York: Berkley Medallion Books, 1966.

———. *Encounters with UFO Occupants.* New York: Berkeley Publishing Corp., 1976.

Mack, John E. *Abduction. Human Encounters with Aliens.* New York: Charles Scribner's Sons/Macmillan Publishing Company, 1994.

———. *Passport to the Cosmos.* New York: Crown Publishers, 1999.

Menger, Howard. *From Outer Space to You.* Clarksburg, W.Va.: Saucerian Books, 1959.

Nagaitis, Carl and Philip Mantle. *Without Consent. A Comprehensive Survey of Missing-Time and Abduction Phenomena in the UK.* Poynton: Cheshire, England, 1994.

Pallman, Ludwig F. and Wendelle C. Stevens. *UFO Contact From Itibi-Ra.* Tucson, Ariz.: UFO Photo Archives, 1986.

Pope, Nick. *The Uninvited. An Expose of the Alien-Abduction Phenomenon.* New York: The Overlook Press, 1998.

Pratt, Bob. *UFO Danger Zone. Terror and Death in Brazil — Where Next?* Madison, Wisc.: Horus House Press, Inc., 1996.

Randles, Jenny. *Abduction. Over 200 Documented UFO Kidnappings Investigated.* London: Robert Hale Limited, 1988.

Rogo, D. Scott, editor. *Alien Abductions. True Cases of UFO Kidnappings.* New York: Signet Books, 1980.

Steiger, Brad. *The UFO Abductors.* New York: Berkeley Books, 1988.

Stevens, Wendelle C., editor. *Message From the Pleiades. The Contact Notes of Eduard Billy Meier — Book 1.* Tucson, Ariz.: UFO Photo Archives, 1988.

Stevens, Wendelle C. *UFO Contact from Reticulum. A Report of the Investigation.* Tucson, Ariz.: Wendelle C. Stevens, 1981.

Strieber, Whitley. *Breakthrough. The Next Step.* New York: Simon & Schuster, 1997.

———. *Communion. A True Story.* New York: William Morrow and Inc., 1987.

———. *Transformation. The Breakthrough.* New York: William Morrow and Co., Inc., 1988.

Sutherly, Curt. *Strange Encounters: UFOs, Aliens, & Monsters Among Us.* St. Paul, Minn.: Llewellyn Publications, 1996.

Turner, Karla. *Into The Fringe. A True Story of Alien Abduction.* New York: Berkley Books, 1992.

———. *Taken. Inside the Alien-Human Abduction Agenda.* Roland, AR: Works, 1994.

Twiggs, Denise Rieb and Bert Twiggs. *Secret Vows. Our Lives with Extraterrestrials.* Tigard, Ore.: Wild Flower Press, 1992.

Walden, James L. *The Ultimate Alien Agenda.* St. Paul, Minn.: Llewellyn Publications, 1998.

Walters, Ed and Frances Walters. *The Gulf Breeze Sightings: The Most Astounding Multiple Sightings of UFOs in U.S. History.* New York: William Morrow & Company, Inc., 1990.

———. *UFO Abductions in Gulf Breeze: The Amazing True Story of UFOs and the Real Visitors from Outer Space.* New York: Avon Books, 1994.

Walton, Travis. *The Walton Experience.* New York: Berkley Publishing Corp., 1978.

Webb, Walter N. *Encounter at Buff Ledge A UFO Case History*. Chicago, Ill.: The J. Allen Hynek Center for UFO Studies (CUFOS), 1994.

Wilson, Katharina. *The Alien Jigsaw*. Portland, Ore.: Puzzle Publishing, 1993.

Index

268 ■ Index